Creating
Strong Kids Through
Writing

Creating Strong Kids Through Writing

30-MINUTE LESSONS

That Build Empathy, Self-Awareness, and Social-Emotional Understanding

Deborah S. Delisle and
James R. Delisle, Ph.D.

PRUFROCK PRESS INC.

WACO, TEXAS

Edited by Stephanie McCauley

Cover, layout design, and illustrations by Micah Benson

ISBN-13: 978-1-61821-845-2

Printed in the United States of America.

At the time of this book's publication, all facts and figures cited are the most current available; all telephone numbers, addresses, and website URLs are accurate and active; all publications, organizations, websites, and other resources exist as described in this book; and all have been verified. The author and Prufrock Press make no warranty or guarantee concerning the information and materials given out by organizations or content found at websites, and we are not responsible for any changes that occur after this book's publication. If you find an error or believe that a resource listed here is not as described, please contact Prufrock Press.

Prufrock Press Inc.
P.O. Box 8813
Waco, TX 76714-8813
Phone: (800) 998-2208
Fax: (800) 240-0333
http://www.prufrock.com

TABLE OF CONTENTS

Part III: Lessons for the End of the Year

INTRODUCTION

As students transition from their early years of schooling to young adolescence, a rush of new emotions and thoughts leads them into a period of uncertainty and exploration. They yearn to fit in and find meaning in their lives, they question their places in the world, and they can easily become self-absorbed.

This transition period is neither bad nor unexpected. Self-examination and self-doubt are important stages of growing up, and they are at the heart of this book. The lessons in *Creating Strong Kids Through Writing* invite students to look inward before expressing their feelings externally. Time and again, we have witnessed students respond in absolutely remarkable ways to assignments that felt personal to them. Not only have students impressed us with their work, but they also have often astounded themselves with their insights and responses. One of our students wrote on top of his writing page during one of these lessons, "I never felt like this before." Although each student will respond differently to each lesson, we have found that providing space for kids to think, reflect, and ponder in a safe learning environment is important for the development of important life skills.

INCORPORATING IMPORTANT TENETS OF SOCIAL-EMOTIONAL LEARNING

Tapping into your students' desire to express themselves in just one part of building strong writers in upper elementary and middle school. When writing is used as part of a larger effort to engage students in the development of social-emotional skills, we believe it is the *students* who do the building, not the teachers.

The Collaborative for Academic, Social, and Emotional Learning (CASEL, 2018) defined social-emotional learning as:

> the process through which children and adults acquire and effectively apply the knowledge, attitudes, and skills necessary to understand and manage emotions, set and achieve positive goals, feel and show empathy for others, establish and maintain positive relationships, and make responsible decisions. (para. 1)

CASEL's design, *Framework for Systemic Social and Emotional Learning*, identifies five core competencies that are essential to the development of social and emotional learning. These competencies are: self-awareness, self-management, responsible decision-making, relationship skills, and social awareness.

Various research studies (e.g., Elias, Ferrito, & Moceri, 2016; Zins, Bloodworth, Weissberg, & Walberg, 2004) demonstrate the importance of incorporating social-emotional learning into the daily routines of schools, including enhanced academic achievement, attitudes, behaviors, and skills. In addition, incorporating social and emotional skills has a significant return on investments (Belfield et al., 2015). However, it is only through the purposeful, deliberate, and consistent inclusion of social-emotional competencies into all curricula that the benefits will be realized. Because we believe that these competencies must be a part of lessons, and not *apart* from lessons, we have designed writing lessons that capture them in engaging activities that allow students to explore, reflect, and apply their feelings and attitudes in constructive ways. Table 1 identifies the primary social and emotional skills that are highlighted in each of the lessons.

Table 1
SEL Competencies Addressed

SEL Competency (CASEL, 2018)	Lessons That Address This Skill
Self-Awareness	1, 2, 3, 7, 8, 9, 10, 11, 13, 14, 20
Self-Management	5, 8, 13, 14, 17, 18, 19, 20
Responsible Decision-Making	5, 7, 8, 9, 10, 11, 12, 13, 14, 16, 20
Relationship Skills	3, 4, 6, 7, 9, 10, 11, 12, 13, 14, 15, 17, 18, 19, 20
Social Awareness	1, 2, 3, 4, 5, 6, 7, 12, 13, 14, 15, 16, 17, 18, 19

USING THIS BOOK

Each of the lessons in *Creating Strong Kids Through Writing* includes the following sections:

- **Objective:** One simple statement that identifies the main thrust of the lesson.
- **Context:** Provides background information on the purpose and intent of the lesson, as well as some hints from our own experience.
- **Social-Emotional Connection:** Ties the lesson to the important competencies and tenets of social-emotional learning.
- **The Hook:** Sets up the lesson in an engaging way to get students interested in the writing activity you are about to introduce.
- **Inviting Students to Respond:** Contains step-by-step instructions on administering the lesson, including, when appropriate, the stages of drafting, revising, and sharing final products.
- **Tips to Enhance or Extend This Lesson:** Allows you to consider gaining larger benefits from the lesson by expanding its scope in depth or breadth. You may consider engaging other classes or even the whole school. Such extensions demonstrate the importance of exploring students' lives in relation to others outside of students' immediate proximity. Additionally, these extensions support the importance of social-emotional learning in a context broader than just one classroom.

Every lesson includes sample responses written by our students that you may use as models, or adapt based on students' ages and grades, to introduce the activity. You may project these sample pages onto a screen or interactive whiteboard or create hard copies for student use. The student samples we have included reflect high-quality writing. Although not every one of our students produced work of this caliber (which may be the case in your classroom), we believe these exemplars may inspire your students to create written products that demonstrate sophisticated and deep thinking.

A WORD ABOUT HOLISTIC EVALUATION

We are cognizant of the many ways in which students may be assessed in terms of their growth as writers as well as their ability to meet grade-level standards. We also recognize that assessment is an area of much debate and continued research, so we leave it to you, the teacher, to establish how your students' responses should be evaluated in conjunction with your school's curriculum and expectations. Our recommendation, however, is holistic evaluation.

Holistic evaluation asks the teacher and student to be partners in making sure that the work submitted is meaningful to the person who wrote it and understandable to those who read it, while simultaneously meeting the goals and intended outcomes of the lesson. If a piece of work is not as strong or clear as it might be, a holistic evaluator would return it to the student with specific questions and comments designed to strengthen the content (e.g., "You went from not making the team in fifth grade to becoming team captain in seventh grade. What happened that made the difference?"). If the grammar, syntax, or sentence structure is confusing, explain to the student that off-the-mark mechanics undermine the story's power and interfere with its flow. Providing an example of a potential improvement will help the student to see what you mean. Also, ask the student to find some errors independently, or ask if he or she needs help from a peer to do so. One important note: Always try to leave room for rewrites. The notion of one draft and then a final product is not indicative of real-life scenarios in which we have opportunities to write, edit, rewrite, edit, rewrite, etc. One of our favorite writing teachers allows every student to rewrite at least one piece per quarter, which demonstrates that she understands the roles of incubation and reflection in the writing process.

If a student submission demonstrates strength in some areas, it is important to comment on those areas, as students need to understand their strengths and be prepared to replicate them in future writings. When students merely get an "A" or "Great Job," they cannot differentiate between strengths and challenges in their writing. Questions such as "Did I use great vocabulary?" or "Did my writing appeal to my teacher?" linger in kids' minds. We find that identifying strengths is not routine and often surprises kids. Thus, they are greatly motivated by it.

It is also beneficial for students to read one another's writing in pairs and sometimes in small groups. Provide guiding discussion prompts, such as:

- This is what I really like about this writing . . .
- This confused me . . .
- I think you can make the writing stronger by . . .
- Tell me more about . . .

Of course, as teachers, we need to know what grade to report. It is critical that students know at the beginning of every lesson how they will be graded. We suggest that effort and the actual process of completing the assignment be strong components of whatever assessment is employed. So, if a letter grade is required in your situation, be sure to let students know what constitutes an A, B, and so forth.

Some of the most meaningful assessments are those designed collaboratively by teachers and students. By sharing the intended outcomes of the lesson, you can engage students in the development of rubrics and scoring guides. You may also ask students important questions such as "What did you learn about yourself as a writer by completing this lesson?" Such insights can help you develop future lessons that meet students' needs.

Students may also benefit greatly when you encourage them to write for a purpose other than receiving a grade or fulfilling a requirement, such as publication in a magazine or blog, recognition in districtwide collections of exemplary writing, or the creation of a schoolwide literary journal. Imagine a student writing an op-ed in response to a community issue! Such extensions help students realize the power of sharing their ideas and the many purposes writing can serve.

If we ever engage students in activities that can be reduced to a single letter or number grade, we will have lost sight of the fact that some of school's—and life's—best learning moments are those that instill lifelong skills and attitudes, such as caring for others or learning how to accept differing opinions. Some activities are inherently worthwhile and demand a narrative response from a teacher. Even a student who earns a "Super job!" comment needs to understand what specifically he or she did well, so it can be repeated in the future. Additionally, guiding questions and comments, such as "I wonder what your writing would look like if, in the future, you provided a specific example to illustrate your point," may motivate enhanced skill development.

BUILDING AN APPRECIATION FOR WRITING

Something within the human condition implores us to communicate. We talk, we listen, we write, we sing, we read, we dance, we cheer, and we use every manner of verbal or physical expressions we can to get others to receive our stories. Think of young children who can tirelessly report what is on their minds. They will often share a seemingly endless series of words and, eventually, sentences—often riddled with lots of details. As students grow, somewhere along the way, they may lose their desire to share or, worse, they may begin to believe that their ideas, curiosity, and ruminations are no longer important. Writing can serve as the important bridge from the unfiltered narratives of toddlers to the deep thoughts of emerging adolescents.

Words memorialized on paper or sent into cyberspace seem to have a permanence not possible with the spoken word. Each essay, poem, lyric, song, or reflection that we produce can last an eternity. Decades—even centuries—from today, a new reader might pick up this or any other book and learn something about the long-ago world. This is why the art of writing is one of the most important journeys we can share with our students, guiding them to mastery as well as joy.

A love for writing and a true understanding of the longevity of the written word take time. To help develop this love and understanding, the lessons in this book contain the following elements:

- **Personal expression:** The voices of our students are of utmost importance. Especially in early adolescence, there is both a need and a desire to talk about one's self and one's views of the world. Providing our students with a legitimate forum to express their ideas not only validates their opinions and insights, but also validates them as human beings. One of the greatest gifts we can give our students is to treat their words and their work with respect and dignity.

- **Open-endedness:** When we assign classroom activities, many students want to know the "right" way to complete them. The age-old request "Just tell me what you're looking for" is the student's plea to grasp not only the purpose of our assignments, but also the preferred format, length, and style. We appreciate these students' desire to be both accurate and articulate, yet, simultaneously, we want them to express themselves in unique ways. A note of caution: If your response to the "What do you want?" question is "There is no right or wrong answer," then please do not mark a student down if his or her response is way off the mark from what you anticipated. Rather, sit with the student to understand his or her interpretation and response. We have found that our students often see the world far more differently than we do. These have been our best learning moments.

- **Integration:** These lessons provide opportunities for students to write from both cognitive knowledge and emotional sensation. This is how social-emotional skills and academics mesh. Not every student is equally skilled or enthusiastic when it comes to putting pen to paper or fingers to keyboard, and some students write freely about their inner selves while others are more reticent. These lessons allow students to engage with writing activities at various levels of depth, knowledge, and response.

- **Fun:** Not just "enjoyment" or "pleasure," but fun! In this era of data-driven everything in our schools, the simple joy of playing around with ideas and words is increasingly pushed to the instructional sidelines. Lessons that are not measurable by some standardized something-or-other are given little notice by those obsessed with accountability. However, we do know this: Having fun while writing and sharing with others can result in some very special, valuable, and educational outcomes. After all, aren't we responsible for growing our students for life?

We always find great joy in students' work. So, help your students explore their hopes, their dreams, and even their fears. Happy writing!

PART I

LESSONS FOR THE BEGINNING OF THE YEAR

GETTING TO KNOW STUDENTS FROM THE INSIDE OUT

OBJECTIVE

In this lesson, you will gather some interesting facts about your students and give them the opportunity to share information about themselves and the lives they lead.

RESOURCES AND MATERIALS

- Handout 1.1: Getting to Know You Better
- Handout 1.2: Sample Response
- Handout 1.3: Lesson Extension Sample Responses

CONTEXT

There is no better way to learn interesting things about your students than to ask them questions about their sometimes serious, sometimes funny, and sometimes confusing lives. This lesson helps you to get to know your students from the inside out, as they reveal in single words, phrases, or sentences those elements of themselves that make them unique or original. We've used this lesson as a stand-alone to help us get to know our students. We've also used it twice in the same year: once at the beginning of the school year and again at the end of the school year, when the students complete the lesson handout a second time without having access to their previous answers. Only after they complete the activity a second time should you return the responses they gave at the school year's start. Watching them compare their two sets of answers often reveals how much a person can change in a few short months—or, conversely, how some things about people stay the same, no matter how much time passes by.

SOCIAL-EMOTIONAL CONNECTIONS

We enjoy teaching this lesson at the start of the school year because many of the following lessons will ask students to be reflective and introspective at an in-depth level. By having them complete this short-answer exercise first, you can open the door to self-expression that can be either humorous or deeply moving. By sharing the sample student response written by an actual seventh grader (see Handout 1.2), you can provide some guidance on how the answers to these questions can be both funny and personally revealing. If you prefer not to share the sample response, that's fine, too. We have found that seeing what another student wrote sometimes gives needed direction to kids who are unsure about what types of things they might write.

THE HOOK

Keeping a straight face, and with no introduction at all, ask random students some direct, yet quirky, questions:
- What's your favorite/least favorite sound?
- What's your favorite/least favorite word?

Some students are likely to say, "I don't have a favorite word," to which you can respond, "Oh yes you do—everyone does. Mine is *hypoallergenic*. Want to know why?" At this point, some students will snicker a bit, while others will wonder where their once-normal teacher went. Gather a few more responses from students, asking for elaboration.

INVITING STUDENTS TO RESPOND

1. Distribute Handout 1.1: Getting to Know You Better. Allow students no more than 10–15 minutes to complete the questions.
2. Once your students have completed their responses, invite them to share in one of two ways: either by randomly selecting ques-

tions and asking for individual responses, or by placing students in small groups and having them share any of the answers they wish to reveal. (*Note.* In these lessons, sharing is never required, just encouraged.)

3. Afterward, collect students' respones. If you plan to revisit this lesson at the school year's end, hold on to these papers so that you can redistribute them to your students after they complete the activity a second time.

TIPS TO ENHANCE OR EXTEND THIS LESSON

- If you have access to your class list prior to the school year's beginning and would like your students to complete Handout 1.1: Getting to Know You Better before or on the first day, then you can simply review their responses early in the school year.

- Have students answer the questions on Handout 1.1 in the way a main character from literature (e.g., Pony Boy from *The Outsiders*) might answer them, or, if you teach science, how a particular scientist (e.g., Albert Einstein) would respond. Teaching history? How would Rosa Parks complete her responses? See Handout 1.3: Lesson Extension Sample Responses for examples.

- If you are going to ask your students to reveal their thoughts and feelings to you as the school year begins, you need to do the same. Teaching is the most human of professions, so any linkage we can make between our students and ourselves helps to build the year-long bond that unites us with our students. So, we invite you to complete Handout 1.1 yourself, sharing your responses with your class.

- If you revisit this lesson at the end of the school year, provide time for your students to compare their two sets of answers completed months apart. Then, open a discussion on what students found most revealing or interesting about the similarities and differences in the responses they gave at these two different times of their lives.

HANDOUT 1.1

GETTING TO KNOW YOU BETTER

Directions: Respond to the following questions using words, phrases, or sentences. Consider which responses you might be comfortable sharing with your classmates and teacher to help them get to know you better.

1. What is your favorite word?

    _____

2. What is your least favorite word?

    _____

3. What is your favorite sound?

    _____

4. What is your least favorite sound?

    _____

5. What would make you as happy as possible?

    _____

    _____

6. What trait or behavior of yours do you most dislike?

    _____

    _____

7. What trait or behavior do you most dislike in others?

    _____

    _____

8. What is your greatest regret?

    _____

    _____

HANDOUT 1.1, CONTINUED

9. What is your most cherished possession?

_____

_____

10. What is your greatest fear?

_____

_____

11. If you could live anywhere, where would it be?

_____

_____

12. What do you value the most in your friends?

_____

_____

13. Whom do you most admire?

_____

_____

14. What is it that you most dislike?

_____

_____

15. What is your favorite smell?

_____

_____

HANDOUT 1.2

SAMPLE RESPONSE

Pav, Grade 7

1. What is your favorite word?

    Blubber

2. What is your least favorite word?

    "often" with the 't' sounded out

3. What is your favorite sound?

    That satisfying click that you get sometimes when two things fit perfectly together

4. What is your least favorite sound?

    The slurping of soup

5. What would make you as happy as possible?

    Feeling that whatever happens doesn't matter because I have everything OK in my life

6. What trait or behavior of yours do you most dislike?

    I am shy around other people who I know don't think much of me

7. What trait or behavior do you most dislike in others?

    Continuous talking

8. What is your greatest regret?

    Not going to India when my grandfather died

HANDOUT 1.2, CONTINUED

9. What is your most cherished possession?

    My talent for writing

10. What is your greatest fear?

    Being kidnapped

11. If you could live anywhere, where would it be?

    India

12. What do you value the most in your friends?

    Trustworthiness and loyalty

13. Whom do you most admire?

    Jackie Robinson and Doctors Without Borders

14. What is it that you most dislike?

    Mayonnaise and clowns

15. What is your favorite smell?

    Garlic

HANDOUT 1.3

LESSON EXTENSION SAMPLE RESPONSES

Possible Answers From Rosa Parks

1. What is your favorite word?

    Courage

9. What is your most cherished possession?

    The knowledge that my actions gave others strength to stand up for their beliefs

10. What is your greatest fear?

    That oppressed people will stop striving for their freedom

12. What do you value the most in your friends?

    Using character, not race, to determine someone's worth

Possible Answers From Mickey Mouse

4. What is your least favorite sound?

    The snap of a mousetrap

7. What trait or behavior do you most dislike in others?

    Tail-pulling

9. What is your most cherished possession?

    My autographed photo of Walt Disney

14. Whom do you most admire?

    The Make-A-Wish Foundation kids I meet in my job

WHO KNEW?

OBJECTIVE

This lesson inspires students to reveal interesting aspects of their lives that will help them get acquainted (or reacquainted) with their classmates and their teachers.

RESOURCES AND MATERIALS

- Handout 2.1: Sample Responses
- A list of four facts and one lie about yourself

CONTEXT

Each of our students is more interesting than we might think. Some of them are expert gardeners, while others are star soccer players. Some have kept journals since they were 5 years old, while one or two may have a goal of riding every roller coaster east of the Mississippi River. Who knows? The only way to find out just how unique our students are is to ask them. With this lesson, you will quickly learn more about your students than you ever thought you could. As an introductory lesson for the beginning of school (or whenever you might get a new class of students), this fun and short writing exercise is one that students will want to complete more than once—so indulge them.

SOCIAL-EMOTIONAL CONNECTIONS

There is nothing more ennobling for children or teens than to learn that an adult in their lives actually cares about who they are and what things about them are important or interesting. A simple lesson like this one gives students a chance to reveal aspects of their lives that are unique and intriguing in an environment filled with trust and acceptance—your classroom. Getting your students to introduce themselves to you and each other in this informal, fun way opens the door for future conversations that delve even deeper into our students' likes, dislikes, ambitions, and fears.

THE HOOK

Have "Five Facts" written on your board as students enter the room—except *one* of the facts is "fake news." For example, the facts could be these:

- The original Twinkie was filled with banana cream, not vanilla cream.
- The U.S. state with the longest coastline is Florida.
- A female termite can have 30,000 babies a day.
- A human's largest organ is the skin.
- When it was first constructed, the White House was gray.

As you read these "facts" to your students, ask them to guess which one is not true. (Spoiler alert: The Florida "fact" isn't true, as Alaska has the longest coastline in the U.S.) Then, ask your students to volunteer any other interesting facts about the world or nature that most people might not know.

INVITING STUDENTS TO RESPOND

1. Share with your students the responses to this activity given to us by sixth graders (see Handout 2.1). Tell students that four of the five "facts" listed by each sixth grader are true, while one of the facts is "fake news."

2. Ask students to guess which responses are lies. (The lies are: Melissa, #4; Clark, #1; and Sara, #3—she plays four instruments.)

3. Next, provide your own list of "facts" about your life, inviting your students to guess which one is not true. This will lead to questions and snickers, as your students will learn things about you that they may not have ever expected to hear.

4. From this point, ask students to write lists of "Five Facts" about their own lives. When they complete this activity—it should take no more than 15 minutes—invite them to share, either with the entire class or in small groups.

TIPS TO ENHANCE OR EXTEND THIS LESSON

- Take a digital photograph of each student and display these headshots along with his or her "Who Knew?" list in an area adjacent to your classroom. If they wish, your students can list the lie on the reverse side of their list. If you have a class website or blog, you can also post students' photos and lists there. Just remember to follow your school's policy regarding student identification (perhaps using only first names).

- Ask each of the teachers in your team or grade level to complete a "Who Knew?" list and reveal their lists to your students. After each teacher reads his or her list, ask students to applaud for the "fact" they think is a lie. Depending on time, students can be invited to ask individual teachers about the four actual facts that they revealed.

- Make this a "family homework" activity by having students ask siblings, parents, grandparents, and others to write "Who Knew?" lists. When completed, each of your students can select one responder to interview, asking about the true facts that make that person's life interesting. Students might follow up this assignment by writing an essay titled "The Relative I Thought I Knew."

HANDOUT 2.1

SAMPLE RESPONSES

Grade 6

Melissa

1. I almost got lost at the Grand Canyon.
2. I hit my head on four metal bars while falling off a jungle gym.
3. I've been to Canada.
4. I have a sister named Stacy who doesn't lie.
5. I know someone who guards the Dalai Lama.

Clark

1. I pulled a fire alarm when I thought it said "free."
2. I cried when my fish got flushed down the toilet.
3. I'm afraid of my grandmother.
4. I can't bend my big toe backward.
5. I named my sister "Rudolph" when she was born.

Sara

1. I'm one of the few girls in my class who has never had a boyfriend.
2. I got my head stuck in a folding chair.
3. I can play two instruments.
4. I'm considering being a teacher for my career.
5. I didn't have hair until I was 3 1/2 years old and then it grew in all white.

VISUAL ENIGMAS

OBJECTIVE

By using the fun and complexity of optical illusions, and creating one of their own, students will describe themselves in creative ways.

RESOURCES AND MATERIALS

- Handout 3.1: Optical Illusions
- Handout 3.2: Sample Responses
- Handout 3.3: Visual Enigmas
- Materials to create drawings (e.g., paper, pencils, and markers)

CONTEXT

Do you know a student who *doesn't* enjoy a good optical illusion? These visual displays that confuse the mind and addle the imagination are a great vehicle to help students explain, in visual form, various aspects of their personalities—both the obvious and the hidden. Best conducted near the beginning of the school year, this lesson complements several others in this book, although the unique aspect of this lesson—using a confusing, visual format—adds immediate student interest. There are no wrong answers in a lesson like this, and imagination is the best tool your students will have to make their responses as unique as they are.

SOCIAL-EMOTIONAL CONNECTIONS

In multiple ways, our students' lives are mysteries to us. We get to see them for a substantial, yet still small, portion of their lives. Because teachers are responsible for the education of so many students in a single school year, the chance to get to know each student individually does not always come easily. Sometimes, we need to "intrude" in a specific, caring, and meaningful way to learn about the lives that our students lead outside of school. This lesson gives the chance to do just that: to help our students put their lives into focus by sharing their experiences.

THE HOOK

Distribute Handout 3.1: Optical Illusions or display the illusions on the board for students to see. Say nothing specific about any of the illusions except that you would like students to examine the pictures to "see what they see." Allow conversations during this time, as students are likely to identify a variety of different objects. Here are some common responses we've received:

1. The capital letter "E"
2. A white question mark or a black-winged bird (like a phoenix)
3. The alphabet letters "A," "B," and the start of "C"
4. A knight riding a horse . . . or a snowman
5. A dog walking through a field
6. You'll get varied responses to the final "impossible figure," as it is impossible to build, except in two dimensions. Prove it by pointing to the top, left circle, and tracing the illustration to the right, down, and to the left. You end up in a "hollow" space, not a "solid" space.

After a few minutes of viewing the illusions, ask your students if anything they've identified for each illusion is the *only* right answer. They should say "no," as each image is simply what one's mind perceives it to be.

INVITING STUDENTS TO RESPOND

1. Ask your students to decipher the terms *optical* and *illusion*. After they've done so, tell them that they are going to create a *hybrid* of

these two terms—something we call a *visual enigma*. Your students will likely know the term *visual*, but *enigma* may give them a challenge. Explain that it is a word with several synonyms—*conundrum* and *quandary*, for example—but an equally acceptable synonym is *mystery*.

2. Tell students: *Each of you is going to create a visual enigma, or mystery, that explains, in both visual and written forms, aspects of yourself that we might not otherwise know about you.*

3. As the quizzical looks come your way, display the two visual enigmas on Handout 3.2: Sample Responses, asking the kids to decipher the two names ("Matthew" and "Mandy") and to read the statements beneath each of the visual enigmas.

4. Tell your students: *Now it's your turn. You will create your own visual enigma using the format provided.* Distribute Handout 3.3: Visual Enigmas, which contains directions for creating drafts of visual enigmas.

5. Once students have created a design that they like, they can draw a final draft (first in pencil and then in marker) on a sheet of paper. They can then compose the five statements that help to "decipher" the person whose name they've just made into a visual enigma—themselves!

TIPS TO ENHANCE OR EXTEND THIS LESSON

- Some students will likely want to do a visual enigma of both their first and last names. That's fine—as long as the given and surnames are "visualized" separately. We've found that putting them together in one visual enigma is too confusing and frustrating for viewers.

- If your students are enrolled in an exploratory foreign language class, talk with their teacher to see if they can complete this activity in the language they are studying, changing their "enigma names" as appropriate (e.g., "Richard" becomes "Enrique"). If they have the language skills, they can also translate their five identifying statements into the language they are studying.

- If you are doing a biography lesson, have your students create a visual enigma for the individual they have studied and write five facts about this person's life. This can be a more innovative way to display what they've learned about an individual than through a typical written report.

HANDOUT 3.1

OPTICAL ILLUSIONS

1.

2.

3.

4.

5.

6.

HANDOUT 3.2

SAMPLE RESPONSES

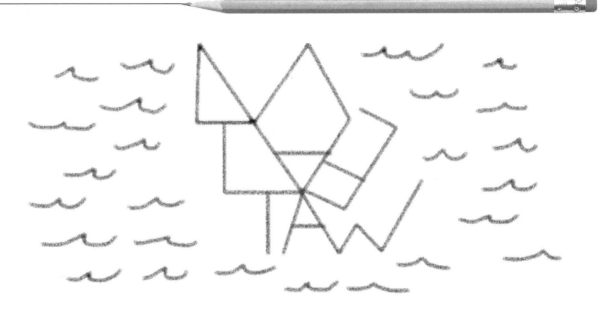

1. My parents are from Romania.
2. I like to fish with my grandfather.
3. I like to read all kinds of books.
4. I like to play pool with my family.
5. I have two sets of grandparents, and I love to visit them on weekends.

1. I used to be a hippie, but I outgrew my tie-dyed T-shirt.
2. I like to try foods that I've never tasted before.
3. My motto is "cool, calm, and collected."
4. I enjoy listening to Old School and composing rhymes.
5. I love when I get love back.

HANDOUT 3.3

VISUAL ENIGMAS

Directions: Create a draft of your own visual enigma. In the box below, sketch an image of your first name with all of the letters connected. You may create several versions if you wish. Then, write five statements that describe your interests, ambitions, quirks, or anything else that makes you unique.

1. _____

_____

2. _____

_____

3. _____

_____

4. _____

_____

5. _____

_____

THAT'S JUST LIKE ME!

OBJECTIVE

This lesson allows students to introduce themselves using an acrostic poetry pattern while also using sophisticated vocabulary.

Note. Several of the lessons in this book allow your students to introduce themselves to others in various ways. This lesson is similar in theme to some of those, but different in focus, as students will use "sophisticated" vocabulary to explain who they are, what they like, and what is important to them. A thesaurus will be your students' best friend in completing this activity. At its completion, you will have a collection of acrostic poems that makes for a great display of the unique individuals who reside in your classroom!

RESOURCES AND MATERIALS

- Handout 4.1: Sample Responses
- Online or print thesauruses

SOCIAL-EMOTIONAL CONNECTIONS

Even the most introverted students, if asked in the right ways, will be willing to reveal what makes them the unique individuals they are. The

29

conversations that follow the completion of this lesson usually open up even the quietest of students, as they divulge aspects of their personalities that may have been hidden. Encouraging courage is a gift that teachers can easily give.

THE HOOK

Before your students arrive, you need to do two things. First, have this acrostic poem written on the board, noting the bolded and uppercase letters:

It's time to write **A** poem
Pi**C**k an interesting topic: you!
You can w**R**ite about your interests,
Or you can write ab**O**ut your personality.
Just choo**S**e some sophisticated words
Tha**T** describe the person you are.
You are more **I**nteresting than you think.
Time to be **C**reative!

Second, have a "plant" in the audience—a student who will stand up and say "Hey! That's just like me!" every time you read one of the following phrases, marked by an asterisk. (*Note.* If you'd like to create your own version from this example, that's even better!)

"When I was a kid, I couldn't wait for Friday afternoons to arrive (*). It wasn't that I didn't like school, it was just that I loved weekends more (*). I'd play baseball (*), eat pizza at sleepovers (*), and, when I got old enough, I'd drive the family car anywhere just to have the chance to get behind the wheel of my dad's old Ford" (**).

Oh yeah . . . the double asterisk means that your "plant" stands up and says, "Whoa . . . that's *not* like me."

No doubt, your students will think that the kid who keeps standing up is either wacky or too overexcitable. Keep the game going by looking annoyed or exasperated every time the student stands up and shouts. When you finish saying the phrases, expose the secret: Your "plant" student was assigned the task of being obnoxious. Now you've got your students hooked.

INVITING STUDENTS TO RESPOND

1. Direct students' attention to the acrostic poem that you wrote or projected on the board (see The Hook section of this lesson), explaining to your students that their task will be to create a similar poem using the format "Just Like _____ (the student's first name)."

2. Ask: *If you were to collect a set of words or phrases that are just like you, what would be on your list?*

3. Ask students to respond with some words and phrases. Then, using a thesaurus, introduce your students to several more sophisticated synonyms to the words they've selected. For example, if a student says he is "kind," suggest "benevolent" as an alternative. If another student says "brave," offer "stouthearted" as an option. Once you've done this with several terms, encourage your students to use a thesaurus throughout the activity.

4. Share the two student examples provided on Handout 4.1: Sample Responses. Ask students to compare the two responses. They may notice that Kara's poem uses simpler terms, while Josh's poem is filled with sophisticated vocabulary. Encourage students to use words found in the thesaurus that tend toward sophistication.

5. Have students complete their poems. When they are finished, you may display their acrostic poems alongside their photos. Almost everyone likes to be recognized as the individual he or she is, and this activity and its display allow students to share their personal traits, interests, and uniqueness.

TIPS TO ENHANCE OR EXTEND THIS LESSON

- Have students complete new acrostic poems using three different prompts: "Just Like I Was," "Just Like I Am," and "Just Like I Hope to Be." These poems can be accompanied by brief essays that link these three phases of their lives: past, present, and future.

- As a class, complete a "Just Like _____" acrostic poem using the name of your school as the central focus. For example, if your school is "Champion Intermediate School," then the "C" might stand for "**C**hild-centered," the "h" for "very long **H**allways," and the "a" for very caring **A**dults."

- On your classroom blog or website, create your own "Just Like Me" acrostic to introduce yourself to parents and caregivers. Invite them to complete this activity at home, using their last names as the common acrostic word. If they are willing, ask their permission to share the poem with other families via your website.

HANDOUT 4.1

SAMPLE RESPONSES

Just Like Kara!

Jolly
fUn to be around
soft Spot for the underdog
Tries to do well

aLtruistic
eIghth grader
loves thinKing
lots of quEstions

Kind
Always wandering
pRecise
black hAir

Just Like Josh!

nonJudgmental
Utilitarian
haplesS (sometimes)
Temperamental

Loquacious
whImsical
Knick's fan
Eerie

Jovial
Obstreperous
Sassy
Organizationally disHeveled

THE PYRAMID OF PERSONAL QUALITIES

OBJECTIVE

This lesson will help students to articulate the essential personal qualities or attributes that help to guide their lives.

RESOURCES AND MATERIALS

- Handout 5.1: Poems to Ponder
- Handout 5.2: Sample Responses
- Article: "Personal Qualities List and Descriptions" by Compatibility Solutions (http://www.compatibilitycode.com/book-resources/personal-qualities-list-and-descriptions)

CONTEXT

All of our students have hopes and dreams about their futures, but kids are often much better at articulating their goals than they are at figuring out how to accomplish them. For example, most people do not become successful writers or athletes by wishing it so; instead, they need to have both specific goals and strategies to achieve these goals that transcend the platitudes of "I'm smart . . . I can do whatever I choose" or "Things will just work out—I know it." This lesson is designed to help your students determine the personal qualities that guide their everyday and life decisions (e.g., dedication to a cause, persistence to reach a self-set goal, or the creativity required to meet any new challenge). Asking students to document what helps them pursue their own dreams is a worthy exercise.

SOCIAL-EMOTIONAL CONNECTIONS

We rarely ask our students to determine which personal qualities or attributes help to guide both their big and small decisions. Too often, it seems our students act on instinct—simply doing what feels right or expedient at the time. Yet, underneath every decision they make lies a philosophy of sorts: a philosophy of life that, if examined, will lead them to consider which decisions best fit the persons they are today and the people they hope to be in the future. By probing into the foundational reasons for why they do what they do, students will come to a better understanding of their beliefs and attitudes about themselves and others. Additionally, students will gain perspectives on others' responses and how those responses are aligned with or differ from their own.

THE HOOK

Before class, display the following jumbled words on the board:
- pohe
- eprcset
- sisterpecen
- rugcoae
- reaf
- nisosap
- enohtys

Ask your students to decipher these anagrams and write their correct responses next to the scrambled words. The answers are *hope, respect, persistence, courage, fear, passion,* and *honesty.*

After the anagrams are decoded, ask students to provide personal examples of times when they displayed one or more of these qualities themselves or saw them in the actions of someone else. For example, a student might say that an older sister struggling with a difficult algebra class showed *persistence* by seeking tutoring help, or another student might say that a parent foregoing one career for another one that better fits his or her interests is an example of *courage.* After garnering a few responses, mention that qualities such as these are common human traits that often aren't as appreciated as they should be. Then state: *So, let's see which qualities guide your own life decisions and goals.*

INVITING STUDENTS TO RESPOND

1. Distribute Handout 5.1: Poems to Ponder, telling students that each poem is best described by one of the terms listed at the top of the page. They just need to determine which term applies to which poem, as each term can be used only once. It won't take long before you discover that your students are frustrated, as you will hear that several of the terms can be used to describe the underlying message of each poem. Just keep your composure (and a straight face) and remind them: *Use each term only once.*

2. Once your students are sufficiently confused, irate, or frustrated, ask them the cause of their discomfort. Likely, they will say something like, "I think this poem is more about courage, but so is another one of the poems." Solicit a few more similar concerns before you make your main point: *One person's persistence is another person's fear; one person's honesty can be another person's courage. No one quality can describe everyone perfectly, can it?*

3. Explain that you'd like students to consider which personal qualities or traits help to guide their decisions and their everyday life interactions. Refer them to two examples (see Handout 5.2: Sample Responses). Mention that the qualities that form the bases of these pyramids ("effort" and "common sense") are the ones that are most important to the two individuals who created them, while the ascending tiers list other essential qualities that also help them to determine which actions to take in life.

4. Mention, too, that one of the most difficult parts of this exercise is determining the relative importance of each of the named qualities, as each one certainly holds a vital role in students' decision-making processes. Composing brief, explanatory comments about why each quality is important to them (as noted on the two student examples) might help students determine the relative importance of each personal quality. (If you need an expansive list of personal qualities, consult the webpage "Personal Qualities List and Descriptions," listed in the Resources and Materials section.)

5. Have students complete their pyramids and explanations. Once completed, these pyramids of personal qualities can either be shared in small groups or displayed in or outside of the classroom.

TIPS TO ENHANCE OR EXTEND THIS LESSON

- If your class is reading a novel, have students choose one character from the book and complete a "pyramid of personal qualities" for this fictional individual, providing explanations from the book's text that validate the qualities as important in the life of the character.

- If you present this lesson near an annual holiday—especially Mother's Day, Father's Day, or Grandparent's Day—have your students complete this activity with a particular older individual in mind, having students name what they perceive as this individual's most recognizable qualities. This completed assignment may be presented to the person each student selects, making for an affirming, original gift.

- Ask your students to consider a possible occupation they might want to pursue in future years and identify the qualities they believe are essential to being successful in this career. Whether their choice is engineer, doctor, rap artist, carpenter, or teacher, they may find that the qualities that help someone to be successful are more alike than not.

HANDOUT 5.1

POEMS TO PONDER

Directions: Read each short verse and then, using the word bank below, select which word you believe best fits each verse.

Word Bank						
HONESTY	FEAR	COURAGE	PASSION	RESPECT	HOPE	PERSISTENCE

1. Saying "yes, and I mean it"
   And "no" when I don't
   While never confusing
   "I will" with "I won't"

   _____

2. The edge of a cliff
   The brink of a tear
   A ghost in the closet
   With no one else near

   _____

3. Baseball in April,
   A rosebud in May,
   A smile on your face
   To begin every day.

   _____

4. Being open to change
   Standing tall by a friend,
   Staying true to one's heart
   From beginning to end.

   _____

5. Believing in something
   So hard that it stings.
   Holding onto a dream
   Until it grows wings.

   _____

6. A fist, not a palm,
   A frown, not a grin.
   An attitude, a look
   That lets no one else in.

   _____

7. Truth, yes, but kindness, too.
   Looking up to one's elders who are
   wiser than you.
   Earning a medal the old-fashioned
   way,
   Giving someone a lift at the end of
   the day.

   _____

Creating Strong Kids Through Writing © Prufrock Press Inc.

HANDOUT 5.2

SAMPLE RESPONSES

Brian, Grade 8

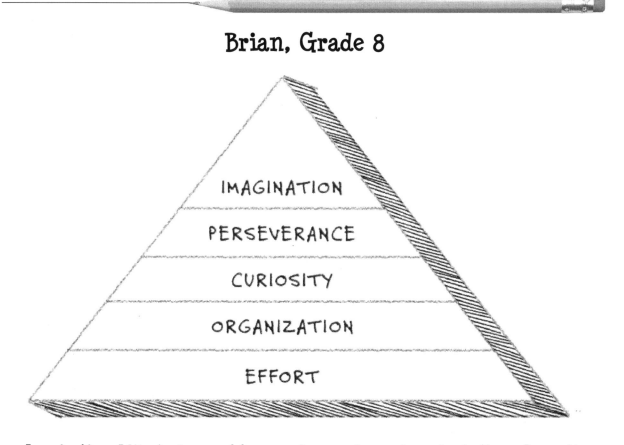

Imagination: I like to dream of faraway places and someday going to them. I sometimes wish I was older, so I could explore the world. But then I think of how much fun it is to be young.

Perseverance: I don't quit at something just because I'm not good at it or mess up the first time. I keep pursuing my goal and trying to accomplish it.

Curiosity: I am always curious about how things work and how they came to be. I like facts and am curious how that fact *became* a fact.

Organization: I like to organize things in and out of school. It makes me feel like I'm on top of things and being responsible. Organization makes things easier.

Effort: I think in order for me to accomplish something to the best of my ability, I have to put some effort into what I'm doing. I have to try hard to be completely satisfied.

HANDOUT 5.2, CONTINUED

Monica, Grade 7

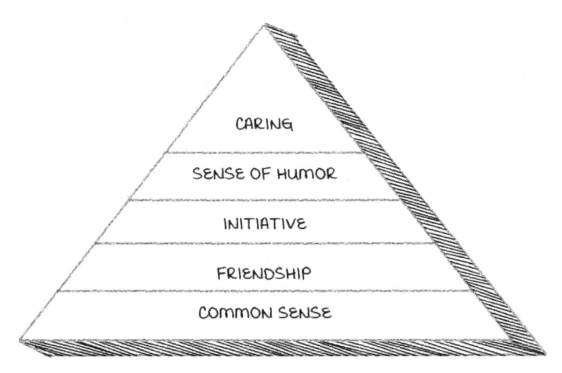

Caring: If you are not kind to others, why should anyone be kind to you? It's not hard to smile or say "Hi," and doing it might actually make someone's day. Caring is definitely something I want on my list of "must-have" personal qualities.

Sense of humor: Life is too serious as it is. Occasionally, you need a good laugh to keep yourself going.

Initiative: Initiative is important because if you don't have it, you will never get anything accomplished. You need reasons to do things, and initiative gives you that. If you always put things off, your life will be harder.

Friendship: Without friendship, I would lead a sad, lonely life with no point to it. All of us need someone to talk to, to laugh with, and to cry with. Without the quality of friendship, all of your feelings would have to be kept inside.

Common sense: This is the most important quality of all, for many reasons. One reason is because if you lack common sense, bad things will hurt you or get you in trouble. If that happens, you could lose things like friends or respect, or do badly in school.

QUOTES FROM THE AGES, QUOTES FROM THE SAGES

OBJECTIVE

This lesson introduces students to quotations from famous people (and others) that can have meaning in their personal lives.

RESOURCES AND MATERIALS

- Handout 6.1: Famous Quotes
- Handout 6.2: Sample Response
- Famous quotation websites (e.g., https://www.quotes.net; https://www.goalcast.com; http://www.quoteworld.org)
- Student computers
- Construction paper and art supplies

CONTEXT

There is a certain magic in quotations. Most of them are short, many of them carry multiple interpretations, and a select few capture personally meaningful sentiments. As an added bonus, quotations provide a springboard for learning about the lives of the famous folks who said them: scientists, artists, authors, athletes, and others. After students complete this activity, your 30-minute lesson might morph into something much bigger—a biography unit, an analysis of a past era that precedes your students' time on Earth, or a collection of personal, reflective quotations for which your students might someday be famous. Let's start with a simple idea: finding quotations that are important to each of the students in your care and asking them to elaborate on their personal connections to these words.

SOCIAL-EMOTIONAL CONNECTIONS

Self-reflection requires that students reflect on how other people see the world or their lives. This lesson allows students to explore famous quotations, reflect on others' lives, predict why they might have said what they did, and even consider why these particular sets of words lived on through history. Students can reflect on these words and see if their own reflections can yield a profound statement.

THE HOOK

Ask students to complete, out loud, the following common expressions:
- "To be or not to be . . . " ("that is the question."—*Hamlet*, William Shakespeare)
- "Ask not what your country can do for you . . . " ("ask what you can do for your country."—John F. Kennedy)
- "The only thing we have to fear . . . " ("is fear itself."—Franklin Delano Roosevelt)

Mention that even though each of these quotes comes from a much longer speech or play, most people recognize these one-liners almost immediately.

Next, display just the italicized portions of the following quotations on the board, asking your students to write down an ending for each quote:
- "*When the whole world is silent,* even one voice becomes powerful."—Malala Yousafzai, Nobel Prize-winning teenage activist
- "*A surplus of effort* could overcome a deficit of confidence."—Sonya Sotomayor, Supreme Court Justice
- "*Don't look at your feet to see if you are doing it right. Just dance.*"—Anne Lamott, best-selling author

Then share the original authors' full quotations. Ask your students if their own endings for the quotations are just as valid as the ones written by the various authors—because they likely are. Next, tell students that the following activity will allow them to explore the words and wisdom of people whose quotations might hold personal meaning for them.

INVITING STUDENTS TO RESPOND

1. Tell students: *You will be using one or more websites to locate a quotation that is meaningful to you.* (Alternatively, if time is short, students may select one of the quotations on Handout 6.1: Famous Quotes.)

2. Once students have selected a quote, explain the rest of the assignment: *Write or type your quotation, in extra-large font, on a piece of paper, and attach this page to a piece of colorful construction paper. Beneath the quote, compose a two- or three-paragraph essay, in which you explain what you think the quotation means, followed by the reason that it is personally meaningful to you.* Display the student sample on Handout 6.2 to guide students as they work.

3. Once completed, the quotes and essays can be discussed in class and then displayed on a wall in a central corridor or bulletin board in the school. If your students' work mirrors that of our students work, you'll want to share their insights with others in this fashion.

TIPS TO ENHANCE OR EXTEND THIS LESSON

- If you want to extend this lesson beyond one class session, there are several ways to do so:
  - Have students write a brief biography of the author of their selected quotation.
  - Have students investigate other quotations from the author of their selected quotation.
  - Have students find quotes from other individuals that align with their selected quotation.

- Why limit your students to writing about "real" people? If your students are reading a particular novel or author, have them select a fictional character, locate a quote from this character that applies to their lives, and do this activity again.

- Most of our students love music and movies, so why not allow them to use quotations from song lyrics or movie scripts if they wish? Some of your more reluctant writers might appreciate this contemporary approach.

43

HANDOUT 6.1

FAMOUS QUOTES

"You have brains in your head.
You have feet in your shoes.
You can steer yourself any direction you choose."
—Dr. Seuss, author

"No person is your friend who demands your silence or denies your right to grow."
—Alice Walker, author

"When I was growing up, I always wanted to be somebody, but now I see that I should have been more specific."—Lily Tomlin, comedian

"The truth is you don't know what is going to happen tomorrow. Life is a crazy ride, and nothing is guaranteed."—Eminem, rapper and actor

"I can shake off everything as I write; my sorrows disappear, my courage is reborn."
—Anne Frank

"The respect of others' rights, is peace."—Benito Juarez, former president of Mexico

"Either write something worth reading or do something worth writing."—Benjamin Franklin

"You don't forget the face of the person who was your last hope."
—Katniss Everdeen, from *The Hunger Games* by Suzanne Collins

"Like I said, I'll be famous one day, but for now, I'm stuck in middle school with a bunch of morons."—Gregory, from *Diary of a Wimpy Kid* by Jeff Kinney

HANDOUT 6.2

SAMPLE RESPONSE

Lori, Grade 8

Someone once asked me, "Why do you insist on taking the hard road?" and I replied, "Why do you assume I see two roads?"

—Anonymous

This quote is about how some people take the easy way out of everything that comes their way. There is a saying that there is always another way to do something. Sometimes, though, there is not. Other times, your own integrity will not allow you to do anything other than the most difficult thing possible. These times come more often for some people than others, but we all reach a point in life when one occurs for us. Some people, myself included, can sometimes not allow themselves to take the easy way out because you would hate yourself if you did. It would hurt you to do anything other than your best. That is the reason this quote is so meaningful to me.

Perfect example: I was making a project for a class. It could have been done very easily. I could have done a sloppy job and just turned in anything and I still would have had a high grade because my percentage was already so high. Yet I couldn't allow myself to do the easy thing. I worked incredibly hard to make sure that my writing and presentation were the best they could be. Quality work earned me a quality grade.

I was proud of that grade and what it represented. My friends were amazed that I would go to so much trouble just for a project. I couldn't explain it to them, but my conscience was satisfied and my inner honesty to myself was intact.

PART II

LESSONS FOR ANY TIME OF THE YEAR

SIX WORDS CAN MAKE A DIFFERENCE

OBJECTIVE

This lesson will allow students to understand that even the briefest of writing can be personally revealing and meaningful.

RESOURCES AND MATERIALS

- Handout 7.1: One Life, Six Words
- Handout 7.2: Sample Responses
- Website: Six Words (https://www.sixwordmemoirs.com)
- Online or print thesauruses
- Blank paper (one 8.5 x 11-inch sheet per student)
- Markers or crayons (at least six different colors per student)

CONTEXT

Legend has it that Ernest Hemingway, that great author whose terse prose has entranced generations of readers, was challenged by a friend to do the impossible: write a complete novel in only and exactly six words. Not chapters, not sentences . . . just six words. Here's what Hemingway composed:

For sale: Baby shoes. Never worn.

He won the bet.

Many years later, in 2006, a collection of Hemingway enthusiasts launched Six Words (https://www.sixwordmemoirs.com) to collect six-word stories from readers. Their idea took off as six-word entries poured in from both famous and ordinary people, resulting in the 2008 bestseller, *Not Quite What I Was Planning: Six-Word Memoirs by Writers Famous and Obscure*, the first of many books published using this six-word format. Newer collections include *Six-Word War: Six-Word Stories From a Generation at War in Iraq and Afghanistan* and *Six Words Fresh Off the Boat: Stories of Immigration, Identity, and Coming to America*. The stories range from the humorous ("Silently suffered his facial hair experiments.") to poignant ("We are still here. Don't forget.") to celebratory ("Thanksgiving dinner with samosas and turkey."). None of the books is entirely appropriate for young children. However, by selecting judiciously from the website, you will be able to share some powerful writing and provide an activity that even the most reluctant of writers cannot resist: completing a school assignment in only and exactly six words. *Just the way Hemingway would do*.

SOCIAL-EMOTIONAL CONNECTIONS

For many students, writing can be an underwhelming experience. Five-paragraph, formula-driven assignments can lead many of our kids to believe that writing is something they do for a grade, rather than to explore some important aspects of the lives they are leading. Many students believe that writing something long and complicated makes it good. That's not always so, as epitomized in this activity. Remind them that even the most memorable life lessons can often be captured in just a few short sentences or paragraphs. For example, it doesn't take a full-length novel to describe how you feel when a friend moves, a grandparent dies, or when a surprise birthday party actually surprises the celebrant. Hemingway's "baby shoes" story is one famous author's example where brevity is powerful. If your students need further convincing on the strength that even a few words can hold, you might want to share one of Hemingway's quotes on writing: "All my life, I've looked at words as though I was seeing them for the first time." Indeed, even short pieces of writing can be potent if the words are heartfelt. By connecting your students' life experiences to the objectives of this lesson—revealing aspects of themselves in six short words—you are enhancing their emotional growth by asking them to consider the many ways that human interactions affect how they feel and act.

THE HOOK

Share with your students some six-word statements written by sixth graders:

- Little sisters make for big problems.
- Plays with dog, dog scratches eye.
- They're mean, but that's their job.

Ask your students: *Why might kids have written messages like these?* Likely, students won't focus on the number of words—six—but, rather, on the intent *behind* the words. If none of your students brings up the fact that the statements were all written in only six words, do so yourself.

INVITING STUDENTS TO RESPOND

1. Distribute copies of Handout 7.1: One Life, Six Words, which contains both the Hemingway story and the assignment's guidelines.
2. After reviewing this handout, including the 12 prompts that students are being asked to respond to in six-word statements, distribute Handout 7.2: Sample Responses to provide some guidance on the types of responses students might compose. Have them note which responses they like the most—and why.
3. If your students are like our students, they will focus on the specificity of the writing as well as the sometimes-enigmatic quality of the responses. Invite them to try to mimic the qualities of creativity, mystery, and innovation that they find most appealing in the example responses provided. Using a thesaurus can add to the quality and assist in another objective: using resource materials as tools of learning.
4. Have students select one of their 12 answers and create a poster (using only and exactly six colors) that illustrates their favorite response they've written, tapping into their creativity and reflection.
5. Display these posters in or outside the classroom to invite reactions from other students, school personnel, and visitors.

TIPS TO ENHANCE OR EXTEND THIS LESSON

- Have students revise their six-word essays several days after the lesson. Some helpful revision questions students may ask themselves include:
  - Do these words express what I really mean to say?
  - Is the image I create with my words specific enough that others will understand what I mean?
  - How do my word choices create a feeling? Is it the feeling I want to create? How could I change it?

- Have your students give you a six-word "exit pass" each Friday on what they have learned from your class during the week. Or, if you celebrate student birthdays, each student can give a six-word greeting to the celebrant. Likewise, if your school has a "Student Conduct Code" that is quite lengthy, have them rewrite this Code in several six-word statements.
- Utilize this activity across disciplines (e.g., Describe John F. Kennedy's life in six words; Write a six-word statement that Nelson Mandela might have said when he was finally released from prison; Develop a six-word description of one of Vincent van Gogh's paintings).

HANDOUT 7.1

ONE LIFE, SIX WORDS

One of the greatest authors in the English language, Ernest Hemingway, wrote powerful novels with complex characters. But in creating that power and complexity, Hemingway avoided flowery language; rather, he wrote simple, direct sentences that grabbed readers and made them sit up and pay attention.

One day, Hemingway made a $10 bet with a friend that he could write a complete, effective story in just six words. His friend took him up on this wager . . . and lost. Here is Hemingway's six-word story:

For sale: Baby shoes. Never worn.

Such can be the power of brevity.

Guidelines

Respond to each of the following prompts with six words. Don't just write *any* words, though. Take time to consider which are the six best words in our whole language that will get your message across. Keep in mind that, unlike Hemingway, you are writing nonfiction responses (personal essays).

After you've completed your sentences, select one to illustrate on an 8.5" x 11" piece of paper using six—exactly six—different colors to express your essay's meaning through a drawing.

Good luck. Have fun. Reveal yourself.

HANDOUT 7.1, CONTINUED

1. Your life as a student

   _____

   _____

2. Your life as an athlete

   _____

   _____

3. Your life as an artist

   _____

   _____

4. Your life as a son/daughter

   _____

   _____

5. Your life, in summary

   _____

   _____

6. Your goals for the future

   _____

   _____

7. Your greatest triumph

   _____

   _____

8. Your biggest defeat

   _____

   _____

HANDOUT 7.1, CONTINUED

9. Your greatest fear

    _____

    _____

10. Your biggest wish

    _____

    _____

11. Your advice to others

    _____

    _____

12. Your advice to yourself

    _____

    _____

HANDOUT 7.2

SAMPLE RESPONSES

Students in Grades 7 and 8

1. Beautiful pain, many stories, never content.

2. Started with promise. Ended with dreams.

3. Two sides. There's more to me.

4. I'm not found when I hide.

5. Great families make for greater generations.

6. Parents will always find things out.

7. Dark, dramatic, disturbing, poetic: my life.

8. Basics for survival: eat, sleep, swim.

9. Spiders all around me. Please help!

10. I want to be an architect.

11. Sometimes, I don't wanna go back.

12. Average, but believing that I'm better.

13. Worked and chiseled but still imperfect.

14. A good mixture: happiness and creativity.

HANDOUT 7.2, CONTINUED

15. Don't let guys ruin your life.

16. Snakes and geese make me cry.

17. Love books, love electronics. Conflicted much?

18. I was lost. I still am.

19. Dreams tightly held. Even when broken.

20. I wonder what this button does?

21. Not always normal but still awesome.

22. Music reaches people. I make music.

23. Raised my sister before raising myself.

24. Sunny with a chance of rain.

25. Six words will never be enough.

26. Please let me grow. Shortness sucks.

27. Change is always a breath away.

28. The end is never the end.

29. Reached for the stars. Then further.

30. So many ideas, so little time.

31. Does hope always work like this?

A CASE OF VOWEL PLAY

OBJECTIVE

This lesson challenges students to compose a letter, essay, song, or poem that omits the vowel most common to their first, middle, and last names.

RESOURCES AND MATERIALS

- Handout 8.1: Thngs Y Knw Mtchng Clmn
- Handout 8.2: Sample Response
- Online or print thesauruses
- (Optional) Books:
    - *The Vowel Family: A Tale of Lost Letters* by Sally M. Walker
    - *Elemenopee: The Day L, M, N, O, P Left the ABC's* by Pamela Hall

CONTEXT

Most of the lessons in this book are designed to be completed in one class period. This lesson—our favorite one—may take two 30-minute class periods, but it will be worth the time. The idea behind this activity started at a conference we attended where teachers were discussing ways to get their students to use more sophisticated or innovative vocabulary in their writing assignments. Because print and online thesauruses were seldom used by our students to increase the range of their vocabularies, we were seeking an activity that would virtually guarantee the need to use these valuable resources. This lesson has become the perfect vehicle to transform unexciting writing into verbal masterpieces!

SOCIAL-EMOTIONAL CONNECTIONS

Social-emotional learning, if done right, leads to a fuller understanding of who you are, what strengths you and others possess, and how to navigate life's inevitable successes and failures in mentally healthy ways. Social-emotional learning also helps to put into perspective the relative value of one's accomplishments. For example, it's hard to take pride in a prize that wasn't rightly earned. So, if you win a footrace against kids who are 5 years younger than you, the gold medal you get will likely be meaningless. Or, if you get 100% on a test of basic multiplication while you are studying calculus, there will be little sense of pride in this achievement. In this lesson, students will be challenged to dig deep into their vocabularies, with the help of a thesaurus, to come up with a piece of personal writing in which they can truly take pride—an advanced repertoire of words that they create to send whatever messages they wish to convey. Part of life is learning to understand what is earned and what is not, what is a challenge and what is not, and what provides satisfaction and what does not. To know these distinctions is important and is one of the foundational blocks of social-emotional learning.

THE HOOK

As students enter your classroom, have this sentence written on the board:

Wlcm stdnts! W'r ll n fr n xctng lssn!

Ask your students to decipher this cryptic sentence, prompting them to state what is missing from the words. It won't take them but a few seconds to notice that the vowels are missing. Then, ask them if they ever write texts or online messages that omit certain letters—for example, *thx* (thanks), *pls* (please), *rly* (really), or *srsly* (seriously). Mention that it is often easier to decipher words when only vowels are missing because there are fewer vowels than there are consonants. Next, distribute Handout 8.1: Thngs Y Knw Mtchng Clmn, and, in pairs or as an entire class, have students match the left and right columns of consonant pairs to make common objects or titles. (The solutions are the following: pizza with pepperoni; Diary of Anne Frank; Los Angeles, California; Harry Potter; macaroni and cheese; South Pole; Walt Disney World; Dr. Seuss.)

Ask your students to write out their first, middle, and last names and determine which vowel is most common to them. Then, without using that vowel, ask them to answer the following question in a full sentence: *What is the title of your favorite book or movie?* Give students a few minutes to respond and share responses.

INVITING STUDENTS TO RESPOND

1. Tell students: *You are each going to compose a song, poem, letter, or essay that omits the vowel most common to your name.* (*Note.* If a student requests using a different vowel, by all means, capture that interest and let the words flow!)

2. Share the sample work on Handout 8.2 with students, noting that the letter "e" is missing from this entire essay, even the book's title and the main character's name. Explain that the student was able to compose an essay without "e's" with the help of a thesaurus. Review with students how to use a thesaurus and distinguish it from a dictionary.

3. Ask your students to choose a mode of writing—letter, poem, song, essay—and create a piece that does not use the vowel most common to their full names. Their compositions could be humorous, autobiographical, or any other genre they choose. In this activity, the main focus is not on the content, but the complex structure of creating a piece of writing that does not include a letter very common in our written alphabet. Make exceptions, if you feel the need, for one or two (at most) words that can include the forbidden vowel.

4. Once students have completed their creations, have them share them with you and their classmates.

TIPS TO ENHANCE OR EXTEND THE LESSON

*   If your students are stuck and need to see more examples of missing vowels compositions before completing their own, visit http://tdc.ds106.us/tdc417 for some excellent examples of student creations that are written with missing vowels.

- Find copies of two books, *The Vowel Family: A Tale of Lost Letters* by Sally M. Walker and *Elemenopee: The Day L, M, N, O, P Left the ABC's* by Pamela Hall. Both picture books deal with the "loss" of vowels in interesting ways. In Hall's pop-up book, the errant letters decide to join the number line instead! Even if your students are older, they will enjoy the connection between their own work and those of these published authors.

HANDOUT 8.1

THNGS Y KNW MTCHNG CLMN

Directions: Draw a line connecting each word or phrase in the first column with the appropriate word or phrase in the second column.

Pzz wth . . .	**nn Frnk**
Dry f . . .	**Wrld**
Ls ngls . . .	**Pttr**
Hrr . . .	**ppprn**
Mcrn . . .	**Pl**
Sth . . .	**Sss**
Wlt Dsn . . .	**Clfrn**
Dr . . .	**nd chs**

HANDOUT 8.2

SAMPLE RESPONSE

Hannah

Th Rd Badg of Courag (The Red Badge of Courage)

Th Rd Badg of Courag is about a young man's trip from acting in ways of a coward to acting in ways of a strong, audacious army man. A youth, Hnry, joins army ranks with aspirations of coming out daring and valiant. Soon, though, Hnry finds out that actual war contains complications his thoughts did not contain in his original analysis.

Th Rd Badg of Courag starts as Hnry joins army ranks. Following his signing up, but prior to his first conflagration, fright and worry that valor and stamina might not portray his actions constantly ran through Hnry's thoughts.

THE ABC'S OF LIFE

OBJECTIVE

This lesson encourages students to explore the mysteries and complexities of life by composing an essay written in a unique, alphabetic format.

RESOURCES AND MATERIALS

- Handout 9.1: Sample Response
- Handout 9.2: The ABC's of Life
- One or two examples of children's "ABC" books collected from any library
- Online or print thesauruses

CONTEXT

When our son was young, he had a bedtime ritual as he was being tucked in: We had to answer one or more questions before we could return to our own nighttime routines. Usually the questions were what you'd expect from a 6-year-old: "If Batman and Superman had a fight, who would win?" or "Can you make me a lunch tomorrow that is all desserts?" One particular night, though, one of his questions took on a deeper tone: "Do you feel the same way right before you're born and right after you die?"

Trust us, we didn't know how to answer him then, and decades later, we're still not sure how to do so—but we didn't want to extinguish the deeply intensive ruminations of a 6-year-old.

Even young children like our son dabble in philosophy before they even know how to spell the word. Questions about religion, politics, equity, and other adult issues permeate their young minds. Sometimes we wish we listened more to their simple solutions, which are often more elegant than the complex ones that grown-ups manufacture. This lesson homes in on the deep thoughts that elementary and middle-grade students often have but are seldom able to articulate. The ABC format that we'll explain has a way of getting students to create imaginative and compelling essays.

SOCIAL-EMOTIONAL CONNECTIONS

Every day that your students come to class, they are thinking about much more than last night's homework or tomorrow's science test. They are wondering if they'll have someone to sit with at lunch or if going to next week's school dance will be fun or embarrassing. They are wondering if the topics they hear their parents talk about at night—politics, family issues, money—are going to impact them in any negative ways. They are wondering what it will be like to be 5 years older than they are right now, or what they will do with their lives once high school is over. As teachers, we don't know what is going through their active minds unless we ask and give them the forum to tell us. Doing so can provide an emotional balm to students whose thoughts about themselves, others, or the world occupy their minds more so than memorizing multiplication tables. That's one of the side benefits to this lesson—not only do you get to read some amazing essays, but you'll also gain insight into the kids who wrote them.

THE HOOK

Before starting this lesson, locate one or two of the many ABC books found in any children's library. Of course, your students are "too old" for such books, but for a few minutes, treat them as if they're not. Circulate the room and ask questions like, "Can you spot the aardvark?" or "Can you almost hear this lion roaring?" No doubt, your students will think that you've forgotten which grade you teach and might roll their eyes at this insult to their maturity and intelligence! Once they've expressed their discontent, tell them that you chose to share these ABC books because they might have been some of the first books students encountered when they were just learning to read. Explain that simple ideas like the ABC's don't have to be limited to the youngest of children, and prove it to them by displaying and reading aloud the first paragraph (or more) of the sample essay on Handout 9.1. Students may not recognize the pattern of writing in this essay, so you may have to explain to them that each sentence begins with a different letter of the alphabet, in sequence—in this case, beginning with the letter "L" and ending with the letter "K." Now you've got them hooked.

INVITING STUDENTS TO RESPOND

1. Distribute Handout 9.2: The ABC's of Life, which gives instructions for how students will compose the essays you are asking them to write. Have students read through the Prompts section and select one question that they would like to answer in writing—in exactly 26 sentences. As you'll note (and you may or may not want to point out to your students), some of the questions are "deeper" than others (e.g., "Can telling the truth ever be wrong?"), while some are more direct (e.g., "Describe the greatest gift you ever gave to someone"). Both types of questions are legitimate, but your students' choices may depend on their comfort level with composing a response that is either "light" or "heavy" in terms of its content.

2. Send your students off to a quiet area of the classroom (or elsewhere) and ask them to select a starting alphabet letter . . . and keep on writing. Be prepared to read some powerful, introspective essays.

TIPS TO ENHANCE OR EXTEND THIS LESSON

- We suggest that you don't have all students read their work aloud, as students tend to zone out after the first few essays are read. Instead, if you choose to have students share their work, do so in groups no larger than three students. Should these triads of students wish for one or more of them to share with the entire class, that's OK, but let the students make that decision. You might also schedule one-on-one time between you and individual students so they can share quietly with you. Again, this should be a choice.
- Some students might read the prompts provided on Handout 9.2 and think, "These aren't very interesting." Give them the option of

writing and answering their own question, such as "What would my life would be like if I lived in another country?"

- If your school has a broad range of grade levels, have your students ask their chosen question to a younger or older student and record that student's response. Then, they can team up to write a combined response using the sequential alphabet format.
- If you want to prove to your students that ABC books aren't just for little kids anymore, get a copy of *The Weighty Word Book* by Paul M. Levitt, Douglas A. Burger, and Elissa S. Guralnick, which uses words like *abasement* and *ingratiate* to spell out the alphabet in complex ways.

HANDOUT 9.1

SAMPLE RESPONSE

Serena, Grade 8

How Have I Changed Since This Time Last Year?

Life is precious. Many things happen for a reason, even though we may not always know what the reason is. Not once will I waste my time doing something stupid, because this year I have changed how I live each day of my life. Often, I think about all of the people I've known who have passed away, and if they lived their lives the best they could each day. Probably not. Quietly, I think to myself every day, "have I lived this day so that if I would die this very minute, I would be satisfied with how I lived it?" Respecting the small things in life has helped me be more thankful than I have ever been before.

Sadly, this summer I was faced with a lot of deaths and a lot of people getting sick and injured. This made me think about some things. Usually, I would just think about the family that it happened to. Various times, now, I think about my family and myself. What would happen if something like that happened to me or someone in my family? Exactly the reason why I think so much about this each day. You never actually realize it could happen to you . . . until it does. Zestful days go by where things go perfectly, and others go by when you just want to have nothing to do with them.

Accept what you have and be thankful for it. Because you never know what the rising sun will bring. Care for your family and friends. Deal with issues you go through each day and try to make them better. Especially, when other people need you. Follow your dreams. Go for your goals. Hold on to the special things you have in life. Increase the happy times in your life so that you can also make the people around you happy. Just remember to live every day to the limit, as I now try to do. Keep these things in mind each day you live.

HANDOUT 9.2

THE ABC'S OF LIFE

Directions: Imagine writing a story that lets your readers know both who you are and what you believe. It's as simple as *A . . . B . . . C.* Using one of the questions in the Prompts section of this handout, write a 26-sentence essay in which each sentence begins with a different letter of the alphabet. Choose a letter to begin with, and then begin each subsequent sentence with the next letter in the alphabet. For example, if your first sentence begins with "C," your next sentence must begin with "D," the next sentence with "E," and so on. The last sentence in your essay would begin with "B."

These rules will make the writing trickier than normal, but don't focus only on the alphabetical ordering. You are not simply writing sentences; you are composing a response to the particular question you select. Your essay needs to make sense. See the Prompts section to select a question to answer.

Guidelines

1. Not all of your sentences need to be complete sentences—some can be phrases or even single words. Don't overdo this technique, but it can be used effectively for several alphabet letters.
2. For the letter "X," you may use words in which "X" is the second letter (like *example*, *axe*, or *oxymoron*).
3. If you get stuck on a good opening word, use a thesaurus for reference.
4. Your work will be displayed for others to see and read, so please do not use names that are real—unless, of course, you are complimenting or thanking that person.

Prompts

1. What do you think your mom or dad was like at your age?
2. What do we owe to other people?
3. Can a person work *too* hard at something?
4. Why do people in groups sometimes do things they would not normally do on their own?
5. Explain how a single leaf falling from a tree to the ground can have an effect on the world.
6. How do you know you are awake and not just dreaming?
7. Can telling the truth ever be wrong?
8. How do you "get away" on your own when you can't go anywhere?
9. What is the weirdest thing that ever happened to you?
10. What is one of the most memorable things someone has ever done for you?

HANDOUT 9.2, CONTINUED

11. What are the qualities of the best teachers?
12. Are all people created equal?
13. Explain the meaning of "innocence."
14. Why do good people sometimes have to suffer?
15. Who among your friends or family understands you the best?
16. Whose hero are you?
17. What is it that makes you unique among everyone else?
18. Describe an act for which you would like to be remembered.
19. How have you changed since this time last year?
20. What one thing have you always wanted to tell someone you know?
21. What is the greatest lesson you ever learned?
22. What question (besides this one) really bothers you?
23. Describe your favorite elderly person.
24. How are you *not* the way you seem to others?
25. If you could live anywhere else, where would it be? Why?
26. Do people have a responsibility to take care of one another?
27. Describe the greatest gift you ever gave to someone.
28. What is the most important lesson you have ever learned from a fictional character?
29. Describe a "masterpiece" you will create someday.
30. When should people control, and *not* control, their emotions?
31. Is it ever OK to break a promise?

NANOFICTION

OBJECTIVE

Using the typical elements of short story writing—plot, character, setting, conflict, conflict resolution—students will compose short, complete essays.

RESOURCES AND MATERIALS

- Handout 10.1: Examples of Nanofiction
- Handout 10.2: Sample Response

CONTEXT

You may have noticed that many of the lessons in this book require less writing, not more. Instead of asking students to complete multipage essays or narratives, we invite them to compose very short pieces that, in their brevity, reveal a lot about our students' character and daily lives. We do this purposely, as we understand and appreciate that many students are reluctant writers, feeling they have little to say of importance to anyone. Additionally, shorter pieces may actually require deeper analysis of word choice because of the limitation of the word count. However, if we can convince even a few of our students that their "writing voices" are worthy of hearing, then they may choose to write *even when they don't have to* for assignments like this. In this era of Twitter, Instagram, and other instantaneous communication outlets, writing anything longer than a couple hundred characters might be considered quaint. We hope that this lesson will help convince your students that a well-executed essay—even a short one—can express messages worth reading.

SOCIAL-EMOTIONAL CONNECTIONS

One thing that has always amazed us when completing this activity with our students is the degree of seriousness with which they complete both their 55-word essay and its accompanying illustration. Maybe having the freedom to write without the constraints of accurate punctuation and complete sentence structure loosens their inhibitions, inviting them to write about personal stories that evoke the "three C's": compassion, companionship, and connectedness with others. Whatever the magic ingredients are, we do know this: These 55-word stories tend to bring out both laughter and "oohs and ahs" from the students who hear them. Also, many of the 55-word stories, once shared, encourage extended conversations among students wishing for more elaboration about the circumstances surrounding their creation.

THE HOOK

Tell your students that today will be a day unlike any other in their language arts class, as they will be allowed—indeed, encouraged—to break some of the writing rules they have long been told to follow. Write the word *nanofiction* on the board and ask if anyone knows what the word means. If they have trouble, mention that "nanoplankton" are tiny sea creatures, while a "nanosecond" is one billionth of a second—quite a short time, yes? So, it should become obvious that "nanofiction" is a short piece of writing rather than an extended essay.

Share the nanofiction examples found on Handout 10.1. After reading the examples, ask your students what elements of writing these short essays contain—plot, character, setting, etc. Then, point out that each essay has something in common: Each one is *only* and *exactly* 55 words. (The titles are not included in this 55-word total.)

Tell students: *Your task today is to compose a 55-word short story—nanofiction—that contains all of these writing elements.* Mention that complete sentences are optional, and that even though the stories are fictional, they must still make sense.

Next, share with your class the essay "Alligator Troubles" found on Handout 10.2 and ask them why they think (or if they think) this is a good example of nanofiction. Is it the realistic details of two kindergarten kids making believe? Is it the surprise ending that, years later, these now-grown kindergarteners are still fighting alligators of a different sort? With any luck, this discussion will assist students as they compose their own 55-word short story.

INVITING STUDENTS TO RESPOND

1. To "prime the pump" for your students' creativity, ask them to begin by exploring the various elements of the story they are getting ready to compose. For example, the setting might be the planet Mars, a fast food restaurant, or a movie theater. Their characters could include a friend, a favorite video game hero, a soldier at war, or a kid at Disney World. Then, ask your students to think about what the story's conflict might be: Is it a conflict with another person . . . an inner conflict in the character's mind . . . a decision that has many possible options and outcomes?

2. Likely, some of your students may still be a bit confused about what to write—and that's OK. Remind them that their first idea might not be their best one, so they should just begin writing and see where their story leads.

3. As they begin to write, walk around your classroom looking for kids who are still struggling with the story's composition. Ask a few guiding questions—*What types of characters are you considering? What settings interest you—a haunted house . . . a NASCAR track . . . a wedding?*

4. Some students will finish their stories within 15 minutes. When they do, ask them to share their nanofiction creations with students who are still struggling for writing ideas. We've found this peer-to-peer sharing often helps get the creative juices flowing. As an alternative, you may have two students work together to compose a single nanofiction story. Sometimes, two heads *are* better than one.

5. Once the writing activities are complete, ask students to share their stories and drawings in small groups. It's not easy to listen to someone read an entire essay or book report, but a 55-word short story? Everyone can tolerate that!

TIPS TO ENHANCE OR EXTEND THIS LESSON

- Have students create drawings that reflect their 55-word stories. Remind them that there are no right or wrong answers to this assignment—merely personal expressions of creativity.
- Complete this activity in relation to an upcoming holiday (e.g., Halloween, Valentine's Day, Thanksgiving). Connecting nanofiction creations to that holiday can inspire creativity and jumpstart writing, especially for younger students who may struggle with topic selection.
- For a new twist on the old theme of "what I did on my summer vacation," ask your students to compose a 55-word short story on what they *wish* they had done during their summer break. This is a great way to welcome students back to a new school year.
- Steve Moss, the editor of a California-based newspaper, *New Times*, has conducted a 55-word fiction contest for many years. Declaring each January 2nd "55 Fiction Day," he invites people of all ages to compose 55-word essays and send them to him. To get more information on this contest, as well as to read some entries from previous years, visit http://worddays.net/January-2-55-fiction-day.

HANDOUT 10.1

EXAMPLES OF NANOFICTION

The Relentless Follower[1]

Two pirates shuffled down the leafy sidewalk, followed by a tall man wearing a suit. The man waited in the shadows whenever the pirates raided a house, demanding candy, but he was always nearby.

"Your dad's starting to give me the creeps," Eric whispered at last.

"Wait," said Pete, "I thought he was *your* dad."

The Family Farm[2]

Five generations of Burkhardts lived and died here. Their tombstones overlook the pond.

Mary and I (the new owners) are renovating the kitchen when three translucent figures appear.

"Welcome, and keep up the good work," they chorus, before floating through the solid stone wall.

Startled, Mary grips my arm. "And if we don't?" she gasps.

---

1   "The Relentless Follower" reprinted with permission of Andrew Looney (1999–2000) of Looney Labs.
2   "The Family Farm" from *The Fool Who Invented Kissing* by Doug Long. Reprinted with permission from FictivePress.com.

HANDOUT 10.2

SAMPLE RESPONSE

Brianna, Grade 7

Alligator Troubles

Kindergarten buddies touring the Amazon on a wooden boat. Suddenly . . . alligators! Thrashing, squealing. Both struggle to stay on, trying to avoid falling into dangerous, gator-infested waters. Oh! The imagination of kids! Years pass, calm waters. Still buddies, but the alligators take the shape of different problems.

FASCINATING FIBONACCI

OBJECTIVE

Students will mix writing with mathematics by creating a piece of writing that follows the Fibonacci sequence.

RESOURCES AND MATERIALS

- Handout 11.1: Rabbit Multiplication Scenario
- Handout 11.2: Fibonacci Poetry
- Handout 11.3: Sample Response

CONTEXT

As with several of the other lessons in this book, this one was inspired by a teacher. She shared with us a poem that one of her high school students had written for a class assignment. What was unusual, though, was that this poetry-sharing teacher was teaching precalculus at the time! Who knew that poetry and mathematics could have something in common?

As this teacher told us, "When I was teaching sequences, I did some online research and came across some Fibonacci-based poems, so I gave an extra credit assignment of writing one. I was overwhelmed by what my 10th graders wrote!"

For those who are math-savvy, the Fibonacci sequence is generated by this rule: $F_n = F_{n-1} + F_{n-2}$. For those who are less mathematically inclined, the Fibonacci sequence is a pattern that has been called "nature's numbering system," and you encounter it every day, as it appears naturally in the petals of flowers, the spirals of pinecones, and the scales of pineapples.

So, even though we developed this lesson thanks to input from a high school teacher, we think you'll find that it can readily be used with younger students like yours.

SOCIAL-EMOTIONAL CONNECTIONS

In the article "8 Reasons Why Poetry Is Good for the Soul," writing coach KM Barkley (2016) highlighted how poetry can be personally helpful to emotional growth. Poetry allows you to break all of the rules of writing you've been taught to enforce. It communicates feelings and thoughts that can be therapeutic. Poetry can help students understand themselves and others by slowing down the world around them, giving both writer and reader insights they might not have ever imagined. The Fibonacci poems your students produce in this lesson might not elicit all of these reactions—but then again, they just might.

THE HOOK

Display or distribute Handout 11.1: Rabbit Multiplication Scenario, and ask your students to determine how many rabbits there will be at the end of the year. After your students remind you that you're teaching them the wrong subject, garner some responses and, if no one can tell for certain how many rabbits there will be after a year, instruct them to read the hints.

Guide students to understand that the number of pairs of rabbits at the start of each month is the following: 1, 1, 2, 3, 5, 8, 13, 21, 34, 55, 89, 144. By December's end, there are 144 pairs of rabbits. Some of your more astute students will realize the simplicity of the rabbit sequence: The way to produce each new number is to add the two preceding numbers. Thus, 1 + 1 = 2, 2 + 1 = 3, 3 + 2 = 5, and so on until 89 + 55 = 144. And, yes, the Fibonacci sequence is endless.

As your students once again remind you that you are a language arts teacher, introduce the following poem, which is written using the Fibonacci sequence with respect to each line's syllable count.

I
Hope
You see
The beauty
And timeless wonder
Of the Fibonacci sequence
Because this is going to be your next assignment

Tell students that it is now their turn to twist mathematics into poetry.

INVITING STUDENTS TO RESPOND

1. Gather together some items that show the Fibonacci sequence on full display (e.g., a pineapple, some marigolds, a pinecone, black-eyed Susans, a Nautilus shell, or sunflowers). If you don't want to bring in the actual items, locate images by searching online for "Fibonacci sequence in nature photos."

2. Using a sunflower as an example, show students how the flower's petals spiral outward from the center in both clockwise and counterclockwise directions. The number of spirals is always two consecutive numbers in the Fibonacci sequence. The same is true in pine cones and in the other examples named above.

3. Once your students understand the patterns of these items found in nature, distribute Handout 11.2: Fibonacci Poetry and review it together. Nine possible poem topics are listed, although your students may create their own topics if these are not interesting to them.

4. To help your students get a stronger grasp on what they might write, share with them the Fibonacci-based poem "The Mystery of the Fib" found on Handout 11.3. Note how the syllables in each stanza follow the Fibonacci sequence by first ascending in number and then descending. Your students, too, might adopt this format.

5. Once students have completed their poems, have them read their poems aloud. Then, post them on your classroom's website or on a school bulletin board.

TIPS TO ENHANCE OR EXTEND THIS LESSON

- Unlike many of the lessons in our book, this lesson may take longer than one class period to complete. We suggest either assigning some of the activity as homework or dividing the lesson over two class periods. The results will be richer and more interesting if students have sufficient time to complete their poems thoroughly.

- Have students investigate and research how the Fibonacci sequence appears in relation to the human body—something called "The Golden Ratio." For example, the following ratios are all identical: the length and width of one's face, the length of one's mouth and the width of one's nose, and the distance between the shoulder line and the top of the head. All of these ratios are 1:1.618—the exact ratio that makes the basis for the Fibonacci sequence.

- Many schools celebrate "Pi Day" on March 14 of each year, so why not also have a "Fibonacci Day" during which students schoolwide recite the poems they wrote using the Fibonacci sequence format? Students can create a slideshow that displays images of the Fibonacci sequence in nature to play during their performances.

- Challenge your students to find more examples of where in our world the Fibonacci sequence appears, using the following examples as catalysts for deep thinking:
  - In the film *The Da Vinci Code*, the Fibonacci sequence is used to unlock a safe.
  - Claude Debussy's "Reflections in Water" uses the Fibonacci sequence in the song's rhythm.
  - The Parthenon in Athens and the United Nations building in New York City use the Fibonacci sequence in aspects of their design.

RABBIT MULTIPLICATION SCENARIO

Directions: Read the following scenario and determine the number of rabbits, using the hints to help you.

Suppose a newly born pair of rabbits, one male and one female, is put in a field. Rabbits are able to mate at the age of one month, and, once conceived, new rabbit babies are born a month later. At the end of the second month, a female can produce another pair of rabbits. Now, suppose these rabbits *always* produce one new pair (male and female) a month from the second month on. How many rabbits will there be in a year?

Hints

1. At the end of the first month, the rabbits mate, but there is still only one pair.
2. At the end of the second month, there are now two pairs of rabbits.
3. At the end of the third month, the original female has another pair of rabbits, so there are now three pairs in the field.
4. At the end of the fourth month, the original female has another pair of rabbits, while the female born two months ago produces her first pair, making five pairs of rabbits.

HANDOUT 11.2

FIBONACCI POETRY

The Fibonacci sequence is nature's numbering system. Time and time again, a plant's leaves or an animal's scales are arranged in this sequence. The number of bracts on a pinecone or the arrangement of scales on a pineapple are similar from one pineapple or pinecone to the next. The Fibonacci sequence was discovered centuries ago, and, as you'll soon learn, it applies to many objects in nature.

In the Fibonacci sequence, each number is the sum of the two preceding numbers, like this: 1, 1, 2, 3, 5, 8, 13, 21, 34, 55, 89, 144, 377, 610, 987, 1597, 2584, 4181. . . .

Just as the Fibonacci sequence creates beauty in nature, so can it create beauty in art.

Guidelines

Your assignment is to use the Fibonacci sequence in the lines of a poem. Take a look at the following examples. The first line of each poem is just one syllable, as is the second line. Each poem's third line is two syllables, and each poem's fourth line is three syllables. The number of syllables in each line corresponds to the numbers in the Fibonacci sequence.

One
Small
Precise
Poetic
Spiraling mixture
Math plus poetry yields the Fib

Math
makes
my head
quake with pain.
Writing a poem
on Fibonacci does the same

This
Is
Far more
Geeky than
Another haiku
Can't we just forget the whole
thing?

This
is
going
to be a
terrible poem
unless I nail a great finish

Here are some ideas for topics, but you may also come up with your own:
1. I learned this about myself as a student . . .
2. I cope with stress by . . .
3. When I want to change things in my life, I will . . .
4. I have discovered that I need . . .

HANDOUT 11.2, CONTINUED

5. I have discovered that I love . . .
6. I'd like my teachers (or parents, friends, etc.) to know . . .
7. When I think of a memory I want to keep forever . . .
8. My life's biggest goals involve . . .
9. What is better than . . . ?

Your poem does not have to rhyme (none of the examples do), and it's up to you to make it either profound and insightful or playful and humorous, depending on which of the prompts you select.

Now.
Get
To work.
You have no
Time to sit and sit
While other students are writing!

HANDOUT 11.3

SAMPLE RESPONSE

Nadine, Grade 8

The Mystery of Fib

1.

I
love
it when
I'm able
to bring together
my artistry and nerdiness
universally
united
nature
and
math

2.

And
yet
is this
but one great
coincidence that
Fib's sequence can be found in things
from flowers to bees
that do not
comply
to
math?

3.

Will
we
ever
discover
if Fibonacci
uncovered the numbers that could
provide the bridge for
the worlds of
nature
and
math?

4.

Or
do
answers
to questions
of such magnitude
remain as mysteries to us—
the idea that
nature could
answer
to
math?

THE LINGO OF LANGUAGE

OBJECTIVE

This lesson introduces students to the many ways in which the English language is actually a composite of other languages across the world.

RESOURCES AND MATERIALS

- Handout 12.1: The Lingo of Language
- Handout 12.2: Sample Responses

CONTEXT

The English language contains more words than any other language—about 700,000. Compare this to Cicero's language of Latin (85,000 words), today's modern French (105,000 words), and even the confusing compound-word jumble of German—about 500,000 words at most—and you'll see that our mother tongue is a lexicon of immense proportion. This is not to say that the English language is an entity unto itself, as it truly is a polyglot: a mishmash of words stolen and borrowed from other older languages. We may be familiar with some of the Greek and Latin influences on our language, but how about Arabic, Sanskrit, or Chinese? These and other languages contributed to our vocabulary. In this lesson, your students will learn the derivation of some of the words they use every day. They will then make a "creative concoction" that uses, in words and images, some of the terms whose derivations they have just learned.

SOCIAL-EMOTIONAL CONNECTIONS

We like to think of our world as more united than it is, yet sometimes we think of countries as too different from our own. We are separated from others in many ways: borders, biases, food types, clothing styles, housing, currency, religions, and, of course, languages. In this lesson, as fun as it can be, we hope your students will come to understand that as different as people may appear on the surface, there is really a common base we all share: a desire to be accepted and appreciated no matter what we believe, what we wear, or the language we speak. In today's classrooms, in which the number of native languages spoken by students could be a dozen or more, it is more imperative than ever to find some common bonds. Sometimes, those bonds can be found in words. Inviting students to learn more about others' cultures can easily transform into empathy and respect for others.

THE HOOK

Ask students to raise their hands if they can speak a foreign language, inviting volunteers to state some words or a sentence or two in that language, followed by the English translation. Then, ask students who *cannot* speak a foreign language to raise their hands. One by one, go to each student's desk, point to him or her, and say one word: *wrong*. When you've made the rounds, return to the front of your classroom and say: *I have proof that every one of you can speak a foreign language.*

Ask the class to answer the following questions out loud:
- What do you say when someone sneezes? (*Gusundheit*, the German word for "health.")
- What is the name of a stringed instrument that you place under your chin? (*Violin*, which is Italian.)
- What do you call a building where you park a car? (*Garage*, which is French.)
- What is the name of a sour, yellow fruit? (*Lemon*, which is Arabic.)
- What is the name of the red stuff you put on French fries? (*Ketchup*, which is Chinese.)
- What is the sport with bucking broncos and bareback riding? (*Rodeo*, which is Spanish.)

85

Tell your students that you are going to help them explore the roots of English by examining common words that come from a foreign language.

INVITING STUDENTS TO RESPOND

1. Distribute Handout 12.1: The Lingo of Language. Review some of the words, and then ask if anyone knows some other foreign words that have made it into the English language. Tell students: *Your assignment is to create several humorous (or serious) sentences in which three or more words are derived from other languages.*

2. Next, display the "creative concoctions" found on Handout 12.2: Sample Responses. Tell students that each of the words written in capital letters is derived from another language.

3. Direct students to the two websites listed on the bottom of Handout 12.1: The Lingo of Language, inviting them to find some foreign-based words that they might like to include in their "creative concoction." (*Note.* Twenty words or so should be sufficient, but you may request more if you include this search as a homework assignment.)

4. Once students have selected their words, ask them to create an illustration that displays one (or more) of the sentences they've constructed from foreign words. Once completed, have students display their work, noting the derivation of each of the words' particular foreign language. They can note these foreign word derivations below their illustration or on the reverse side of the page they've created.

TIPS TO ENHANCE OR EXTEND THIS LESSON

- Incorporate world geography by having students locate on a world map the countries of origin of the words they have selected. Have students draw the flags of the nations from which their words derive, and place these on a streamer around your classroom, under the banner headline, "One world, many languages."

- Examine how the English language continues to evolve by looking at the annual list of new words accepted into the Oxford English Dictionary (see https://public.oed.com/updates). Some recent inclusions are *hangry*, *burp cloth*, and *commodify*. Post these new words on your school's website, asking students to try to decipher their definitions. Ask your students for suggestions of what word *should* exist, and then have them create a "future dictionary" for your classroom or school.

- Students' ethnic backgrounds are likely to be very diverse. Ask your students to compile a list of "terms of endearment" they give to their grandparents or other family members. For example, "grandma" might actually emanate from *grand mere* (French), *yiayia* (Greek), or *abuela* (Spanish).
- If your students are intrigued by etymology, have them explore various etymology websites, such as Wordorigins.org (http://www.wordorigins.org), Wordwizard (http://www.wordwizard.com), or Word Spy (https://wordspy.com). Language's derivations can be as fun as they are intriguing, as these sites will show you.

HANDOUT 12.1

THE LINGO OF LANGUAGE

The English language has borrowed heavily from older languages that are spoken across the world. Here are just a few examples of common English words, organized by their language of origin:

Arabic: algebra, genie, lemon, magazine, mattress, sherbet, sofa, tariff, zero
Australian Aborigine: boomerang, kangaroo, koala
Chinese: gung ho, ketchup, tea
French: beret, cadet, camouflage, chef, garage, pastel, sabotage, toupee
German: delicatessen, dumb, kindergarten, nickel, quartz, waltz
Greek: circus, eureka, genesis, phobia
Hebrew: amen, cinnamon, jubilee, rabbi
Italian: balcony, ballroom, bravo, pasta, studio, trombone
Japanese: kimono, soy, teriyaki, tycoon
Latin: alibi, axis, extra, integer, ratio, trivia
Sanskrit: bandana, cheetah, dungarees, polo, shampoo
Spanish: banana, canyon, cocoa, macho, poncho, rodeo, tomato, tortilla
Various Native American Languages: canoe, moccasin, moose, powwow, tomahawk

As you can see, English is like a jigsaw puzzle of other languages combined to create a new language spoken by billions of people worldwide. Called *loanwords* by etymologists, or those who study words for a living, these borrowed words are used by people every day, in almost every sentence we speak and read.

Guidelines

Your assignment is to create several humorous (or serious) sentences in which three or more words are derived from other languages. The following websites will help you discover more of the unique words used in the English language:

- KryssTal Borrowed Words in English (http://www.krysstal.com/borrow.html): This site explores how 146 languages have given us words we use in everyday conversations and written communications.
- Online Etymology Dictionary (https://www.etymonline.com): Curious about a particular word's origin? Search this site, and you'll discover its original language and meaning.

HANDOUT 12.2

SAMPLE RESPONSES

The POLKA player hit the CAMOUFLAGED TAPIR instead of the GONG.

The TOBOGGAN-riding, TOMAHAWK-throwing MOOSE was wearing MOCCASINS while SQUASHING the SKUNK.

GOOBER Gary ate BROCCOLI while doing the WALTZ with a DUMB DACHSHUND who smelled like LIMBURGER TORTILLAS.

The KANGAROO said "AMEN" before eating his GUMBO with KETCHUP.

TABULA RASA

OBJECTIVE

This lesson allows students to explore their interests, hopes, fears, and futures by completing open-ended statements.

RESOURCES AND MATERIALS

- Handout 13.1: Sample Responses
- Handout 13.2: Tabula Rasa

CONTEXT

Tabula rasa is a Latin term that translates to "blank slate." Some philosophers, like John Locke, used this term to describe what the human mind is like before ideas have been imprinted on it by outside forces, such as interactions with others and sensory experiences. Of course, the students in your classroom are not entirely blank slates, as their lived experiences have caused them to hold certain beliefs, to value particular ideas, and to eschew those parts of the world that they find distasteful. In this lesson, your students will be encouraged to express their views on many life situations and conditions they may be confronting. By jotting down the first thoughts that come to mind as they complete these open-ended prompts, students will gain a more nuanced view of the experience of living in a world full of contradictions and inconsistencies.

SOCIAL-EMOTIONAL CONNECTIONS

Whether your students are 9 or 14 years old, they relish the chance to talk about themselves: who they are, who they hope to become, and how their lives might turn out as they mature. This lesson allows open discussion of myriad personal and societal issues that your students may be pondering but seldom have the chance to discuss at school. In a classroom that is respectful of different views and opinions, this lesson will help cement a bond between you and the students you are teaching.

THE HOOK

Prior to class, write several of the following questions on the board:
- What is your favorite time of day? Why?
- If you could go anywhere in the world, where would it be? Why there?
- Have you ever moved from one town to another one? What was that like?
- What superpower would you like to have? How would you use it?
- What do you think about when you can't fall asleep?
- If you were a parent, what would be your top two rules for your kids? Why?
- What is one of the funniest things that ever happened to you?

In groups of three or four students, have each student select one of these questions to answer orally to other group members. After 5 minutes, ask if anyone wants to share a response. Get ready for giggles and "aww, that's so sweet," depending on the content of students' responses.

At this point, explain to them what the term *tabula rasa* means and ask if they believe this philosophy is true for them. Say: *Well, you certainly aren't blank slates anymore, so let's get into an activity that will reveal just how full your slate really is.*

INVITING STUDENTS TO RESPOND

1. Distribute Handout 13.1: Sample Responses, which includes several open-ended prompts and our own students' responses to

them. After allowing students a few minutes to read, ask them how they would respond to these statements.

2. Next, ask your students to complete the incomplete statements found on Handout 13.2: Tabula Rasa, but give them this instruction: *I want you to write the first thing that comes to your mind. Do not overthink your answers. Your first thoughts will likely be your most honest thoughts.*

3. After 15 minutes of writing time, go around the room, stopping at individual students' desks, repeating one of the prompts (e.g.,"When I consider my future . . . "), asking them to share the answer they gave. Go to several more students' desks, reciting the same prompt.

4. Then, select another prompt and ask different students to share how they responded.

5. As class ends, ask your students this question: *What did we just learn about ourselves and each other by completing this lesson?*

TIPS TO ENHANCE OR EXTEND THIS LESSON

- Have students create a series of "cartoon bubbles" that include an original prompt with several student responses displayed below it. This would look great on a bulletin board for your classroom.

- Whatever grade level you teach, have your students ask these same questions to a class of younger or older students in your school. Once they have compiled the responses of these other children, lead a discussion as to how similar and different the responses are from kids of different ages. Students could also ask their parents, caregivers, or grandparents to complete the same sentence stems, and then discuss their responses in class.

- If your students really enjoyed this lesson, ask them to write their own sentence stems on topics or issues of concern to them. Using a round-robin format, have each of your students pose the incomplete sentence to classmates, inviting them to respond orally.

SAMPLE RESPONSES

If I could change one thing about my life . . .
- I would be more open-minded and accepting of others.
- I'd want my parents to have the lives they always wanted.
- I would be taller.
- I would spend less time in school.
- I wouldn't be sad anymore.
- I wouldn't move so many times.

If I could change one thing about my world . . .
- Every kid would have a parent close by.
- No one would be hungry.
- I would make people be kinder toward one another.
- I would want more worldwide peace.
- I'd make the oceans clean again.
- Everyone could be who they are without ridicule from others.
- I wouldn't allow news reporters to share horrible stories.

If I could convince my teachers of one thing . . .
- Please stop telling me to work harder!
- It would be that yelling accomplishes nothing.
- I would get them to eliminate all the busywork I have to do.
- I would have them celebrate little things, like the first snow, with a cup of hot chocolate.
- I don't have a quiet place to study at home.

When I consider my future . . .
- I think medicine, medicine, medicine!
- I have no idea what I want to do, because so many things interest me.
- I wonder if having kids of my own is a good idea.
- I don't know whether I'm more scared or excited.
- I want to do something special for my grandmother because she has been so kind to me.

HANDOUT 13.2

TABULA RASA

Directions: For each of the following prompts, respond with the first thing that comes to mind. Your responses to these open-ended statements will give you a glimpse into who you are, who you might become, what (and who) is important to you, what you're concerned about, and what captures your imagination and attention. None of your answers is wrong if you're honest.

1. I do best in school when . . .

_____

_____

2. I do worst in school when . . .

_____

_____

3. If only people would ask me, I'd tell them . . .

_____

_____

4. Most of my friends expect me . . . .

_____

_____

5. The most interesting aspect of my life is . . .

_____

_____

6. A song title that describes me is . . .

_____

_____

7. If I could be a movie character, I would be . . .

_____

_____

HANDOUT 13.2, CONTINUED

8. My social life . . .

_____

_____

9. My greatest joy . . .

_____

_____

10. My biggest fear . . .

_____

_____

11. My hope for my parents . . .

_____

_____

12. In 20 years . . .

_____

_____

13. The emotion that I value the most in myself is . . .

_____

_____

14. I laugh loudest when . . .

_____

_____

15. If my friends were to describe me in one word, it would be . . .

_____

_____

TWO SIDES OF THE SAME COIN

OBJECTIVE

In this lesson, students consider times in their lives when they supported others or others supported them, by asking parallel questions seen from opposite perspectives.

RESOURCES AND MATERIALS

- Handout 14.1: Sample Responses
- Handout 14.2: Two Sides of the Same Coin
- Coins from several different nations (e.g., U.S. coins, pesos, Euros, etc.)
- Article: "15 Mesmerizing Coin and Bill Designs From Around the World" by Kevin Whipps (https://creativemarket.com/blog/coin-and-bill-designs)
- Materials to create drawings (e.g., paper, pencils, and markers)
- Yarn or fishing line to hang drawings

CONTEXT

Every day your students either help someone else or have someone else help them. These moments can happen in the smallest way, like assisting a classmate with a tough homework assignment, or on a grander scale, like standing up for someone who is getting bullied by others. As expressed by Andrea Ramsey (2018), sometimes you are a roof to another person, and sometimes another person is a roof for you (see the blog post "Profundity in Portland" at https://www.andrearamsey.com/profundity-in-portland for more). In this lesson, students will consider times when they were both the giver and the recipient of some type of assistance or care that helped make their day—or someone else's—just a little bit better.

We think back fondly to when our son, in first grade, was so excited that we bought him the largest box of Crayola crayons (at that time, 64 colors). A few weeks later he returned home without them. He explained to us that he gave them to a classmate because the teacher kept complaining that this student wasn't prepared to color. Our son said to us, "I knew he would never have a box of crayons of his own, and I knew you wouldn't get mad at me for giving him something that I had. You don't have to buy me that large box. I'll take a smaller one." (Yes, we did buy him another large box of crayons, and that student became one of his best friends.) A lesson for us all.

SOCIAL-EMOTIONAL CONNECTIONS

Most children are natural caregivers—they want to help friends, family, pets, and even strangers feel safe, comfortable, or valued. On the other side of the coin, children often become the recipient of another person's concern. Whatever the extent of the caring, the result is the same: a human connection that unites two people. Asking students to think about specific instances in which they were someone's "roof" or someone was a "roof" to them can help them examine and appreciate these shared courtesies (Ramsey, 2018).

THE HOOK

Come to class prepared with a pocketful of coins from different nations. As students arrive, hand each of them a coin and ask them to examine it. Whether the coins are familiar or foreign to them, ask your students to explore the intricacies of each coin's design. Some coins will contain natural or constructed landmarks, others will show important people in that country's history, and still more will depict plants or animals (e.g., Canada's dollar coin pictures a loon, Egypt's one pound coin contains an image of King Tut, and the new British pound is a 12-sided beauty featuring images of the Queen and her crown). For more examples of currency, see the article "15 Mesmerizing Coin and Bill Designs From Around the World."

After hearing a few students describe why they believe their coins were designed as they were, ask them if they've ever heard the expression, "There are two sides to every coin." How do they interpret this statement? Once they have offered a few responses, tell your students that they are going to design their own coin that will not only display some original artwork, but will also use words to describe two sides of a similar situation.

INVITING STUDENTS TO RESPOND

1. Share with your students Handout 14.1: Sample Responses. Explain that each side of the coin is organized around a theme: either giving help or receiving help. Discuss if they've ever experienced situations similar to the ones expressed by this student.

2. Using Handout 14.2: Two Sides of the Same Coin, ask students to write down two or more statements in each of the two categories—how they improved someone's life and how someone else improved theirs. Next, on a piece of construction paper, have each student cut out a dinner-plate size circle, and, following the example coin on Handout 14.1, write an example of helping on one side and an example of receiving help on the other.

3. Give students time to decorate the coin with hand-drawn illustrations or figures that correspond to the messages they've written.

4. When the coins are complete, hang them from the ceiling using long pieces of yarn or fishing line.

TIPS TO ENHANCE OR EXTEND THIS LESSON

- If you'd like to incorporate current events in this lesson, have your students select a local, national, or world issue they consider important. Ask them to design a coin that addresses the problem on one side of the coin and a solution to the issue on the reverse side of the coin.

- Commemorative coins are issued by governments and other institutions routinely to honor an event (e.g., the first Moon landing) or to celebrate (e.g., Summer or Winter Olympics). Ask your students to think of one achievement, in their personal lives or the lives of others, that deserves its own commemorative coin, and then design it.

- Invite your students to design and create a paper coin to thank or recognize a friend or relative. One side of this coin can contain images, while the other side of the coin can express in words why this person deserves to be honored.

HANDOUT 14.1

SAMPLE RESPONSES

Side One: Describe a time when someone's actions improved your life.

- When I moved to a new school, a kid who had only moved in recently himself sat with me at lunch when I was sitting alone.
- When I forgot my crayons at home in first grade, another kid let me share hers. At the end of the day she told me to keep them in case I ever forgot my crayons again.
- I was mowing our lawn on a really hot day, and the kid next door was selling lemonade. He came over and gave me a free glass because he said I looked hot and thirsty.
- When I walked out of the school bathroom, I didn't notice that I had a trail of toilet paper attached to my shoe. A kid I didn't even know said "psst . . . check your feet."

HANDOUT 14.1, CONTINUED

Side Two: Describe a time when your actions improved someone else's life.

- My mom was having a real tough day after she heard that her favorite uncle had died, so I took my allowance money and treated her to ice cream.
- I asked my teacher if, instead of going to study hall, I could tutor a younger kid who needed help. I've been doing that now for two months.
- Getting ready for gym class, a kid was having lots of struggles with his lock and looked panicked. I went over and showed him how to open it quickly.
- Our field hockey team lost its final game of the season and we were all sad. I suggested to everyone that we take advantage of a nearby mud puddle and just jump in it and get messy. That made us all feel better.

HANDOUT 14.2

TWO SIDES OF THE SAME COIN

Directions: For each of the following prompts, write two or three responses.

Describe a time when someone's actions improved your life.

1. _____

_____

2. _____

_____

3. _____

_____

Describe a time when your actions improved someone else's life.

1. _____

_____

2. _____

_____

3. _____

_____

Create a Coin Drawing

Now, on a piece of construction paper, cut out a dinner-plate size circle, and write an example of helping on one side and an example of receiving help on the other. You may decorate the coin with hand-drawn illustrations or figures that correspond to the messages you wrote.

SCIENCE FACT AND FICTION

OBJECTIVE

After learning the *actual* reasons why certain things happen in our world, students will use their creativity to invent *fake* reasons, inviting classmates to explore both facts and fantasy in the world we all inhabit.

RESOURCES AND MATERIALS

- Handout 15.1: Can You Fry an Egg on a Hot Sidewalk?
- Handout 15.2: Science Fact or Fiction?
- Website: "Everyday Mysteries" by the Library of Congress (https://www.loc.gov/rr/scitech/mysteries)

CONTEXT

Most of the lessons in this book relate specifically to English language arts. However, some of your students may be more interested in the technical and scientific sides of things. This lesson, even though it contains a writing component, is meant for them. After reading about some everyday mysteries from the fields of physics, astronomy, zoology, and other scientific or technical areas, your students will produce a "plausible lie" that gives a fake explanation of the phenomena that they have just investigated. Students' goal is to write a lie that sounds so believable that others might have difficulty distinguishing science fact from science fiction.

SOCIAL-EMOTIONAL CONNECTIONS

One of the many things that unites us as people is our ability to laugh, to find humor in everyday occurrences, and to share that humor with others. Having some laughs while inventing a creative lie will be a social boon to students whose natural inclination tends toward the imaginative or the outright absurd! Social learning involves the often underappreciated importance of humor, absurdity, and idea invention in creating or transforming personal relationships. This activity promotes all of these important social elements.

THE HOOK

Before your students arrive, write these questions on the board:
- Is it true that no two snow crystals are alike?
- Is it possible to domesticate a zebra?
- Why does chopping an onion make some people cry?
- Why do people yawn?

Gather students in small groups and have them hypothesize the answers to these questions. Then, reveal the actual reasons, which can be found on the "Everyday Mysteries" webpage from the Library of Congress (see Resources and Materials). For instance, the question of whether or not zebras can be domesticated has an easy answer: No, they cannot. Why not? Because zebras are unpredictable and known to attack people. Further, in order for any animal to be domesticated, it must have a good disposition and not be prone to panic attacks—zebras have neither of these qualities. After telling this to your students, ask them, still in small groups, to invent a plausible-sounding false answer that gives reasons for how zebras *can* be domesticated.

Tell your students that they are about to become "liars for a day" by creating fake answers to scientific questions after they have learned the genuine answers.

INVITING STUDENTS TO RESPOND

1. Share with students the explanations on Handout 15.1: Can You Fry an Egg on a Hot Sidewalk? After students read both explanations, ask them which one they believe to be "science fact" and which one they believe to be "science fiction." Students should offer brief explanations for their selections. Students should recognize that both answers sound plausible because neither is so far-fetched that it sounds ridiculous. Emphasize that as they are creating their own "science fiction" responses, they must be mindful to make them somewhat believable.

2. Next, distribute Handout 15.2: Science Fact or Fiction? In pairs or small groups, have your students visit the "Everyday Mysteries" website and explore several of the dozens of questions found on the handout and on website. After doing so, instruct students to select one question of interest to all group members, read and write out a summary of the "science fact" answer, and then create a "science fiction" response that sounds feasible.

3. These questions and answers can then be displayed on a "Science Fact or Fiction?" bulletin board in your classroom.

TIPS TO ENHANCE OR EXTEND THIS LESSON

- The "Everyday Mysteries" website not only gives answers to scientific oddities, but also provides additional resources for students who are interested in doing further investigation into a particular question or topic of interest. Encourage this interest.

- Science isn't the only domain to be filled with mysteries—or lies! If you want to expand this lesson to include social studies, seek out a couple of books (e.g., the best-selling *Legends, Lies, and Cherished Myths of American History* by Richard Shenkman and *Whoppers: History's Most Outrageous Lies and Liars* by Christine Seifert). Note that some of the tales told are meant for older students, so use these books judiciously.

- Have students ask their parents or grandparents about any "family fact" or "family fiction" anecdotes from their early years. Did 3-year-old Tommy actually run away from home to look at new cars? Did Alyse really eat white glue when she was little because she thought it was candy? Legends abound in families as much as they do in science and history.

HANDOUT 15.1

CAN YOU FRY AN EGG ON A HOT SIDEWALK?

Directions: Determine which response below is *science fact* and which one is *science fiction*. How do you know?

Can you fry an egg on a hot sidewalk?

Answer A: Actually, frying an egg on a hot sidewalk is pretty easy to do. It may take a while, but if the temperature is more than 95°F and the sun is blazing down on the cracked egg, it will begin to fry in about 40 minutes. The time is shorter if the sidewalk is paved in black.

Answer B: No, despite many stories about frying eggs on sidewalks, it almost never happens. A cracked egg needs to get to 158°F to cook, and even the hottest black pavement seldom gets above 145°F. Also, when you crack an egg on a sidewalk, it lowers the sidewalk temperature enough that an egg won't cook.

NAME: _____ DATE: _____

SCIENCE FACT OR FICTION?

Directions: With your group or partner, explore the sometimes simple and sometimes complicated reasons why things are as they are in science. Using the website "Everyday Mysteries" by the Library of Congress (https://www.loc.gov/rr/scitech/mysteries), find answers to several questions, such as the following:

1. Can it rain frogs?
2. Is it true that no two snow crystals are alike?
3. What causes the sound of thunder?
4. Why is the ocean blue?
5. Can you build a house made of straw?
6. Who invented the toothbrush?
7. Why does chopping an onion make some people cry?
8. Why does pepper make some people sneeze?
9. Why do you yawn?
10. How do fortunes get into fortune cookies?
11. Why do bats live in caves?
12. Why do you see your breath when it's cold outside?

Select one question of interest to all group members, read and write out a summary of the "science fact" answer, and then create a "science fiction" response that sounds feasible.

PART III

LESSONS FOR THE END OF THE YEAR

THE BOOK OF REALLY BIG QUESTIONS

OBJECTIVE

This lesson engages students in conversations about their lives, the lives of others, and the status of our world through open-ended questions that will tap into their interests, concerns, assumptions, and beliefs.

RESOURCES AND MATERIALS

- Handout 16.1: Really Big Questions
- Handout 16.2: Sample Responses

CONTEXT

We've always loved engaging our students in conversations that incorporate questions with multiple answers. Whether the questions involve something serious (e.g., "What do you believe your life will be like in 20 years?"), humorous (e.g., "What is the worst-looking outfit you ever wore?"), or simply quizzical (e.g., "If you had to put one item into a time capsule that would be opened in 100 years, what object would best represent today's world?"), the variety of responses we receive always get us thinking about just how curious and knowledgeable our students are and how openly they wish to share their views and opinions.

We put this lesson together after reading several years' worth of "Big Questions" posed monthly in *The Atlantic* since 2013 (https://www.the atlantic.com/magazine/category/big-question). Because many of the questions in this decidedly liberal magazine deal with politics, religion, and other adult topics, we are not suggesting that you use all of the questions with your students. However, some of the questions are definitely appropriate for kids (e.g., "What fictional school would you most like to attend?" and "Which book should be required reading for everyone on Earth?"). So, when you combine some of *The Atlantic*'s "Big Questions" with others we've designed for this lesson, you will have a fabulous collection of conversation starters for your students.

SOCIAL-EMOTIONAL CONNECTIONS

Associate Supreme Court justice Oliver Wendell Holmes once said that "pretty much all the honest truth-telling that is in this world is done by children." Dr. Seuss, in one of his countless tributes to the integrity of childhood, wrote that "a person's a person, no matter how small." Both of these quotes point to the emotional importance of being listened to and having one's thoughts and opinions respected and valued. By providing our students the chance to express their views on topics both frivolous and weighty, we are proving that we care about them as the people they are today, not just the adults they will grow to become.

THE HOOK

Place students in groups of three or four and tell them they are going to answer a few questions in quick succession in a round-robin fashion. Start with the question "Which fictional school would you most like to attend?" No doubt, you'll hear Hogwarts School from the Harry Potter series of books, or perhaps Walkerville Elementary from *The Magic School Bus*. You might even get a response about an individual teacher, such as Merlin, King Arthur's tutor, or Dewey Finn, the extraordinary teacher in the film *School of Rock* who convinced kids who thought they had nothing to offer that they were wrong. Next, ask two more questions:

- If emotions could talk, which two would have the most to say to each other?
- Which inanimate object in your house would be the most fun to spend time with if it were alive?

Tell your students that they will be creating a book called *The Book of Really Big Questions* containing their answers to multiple open-ended queries that are sometimes serious and sometimes wacky.

INVITING STUDENTS TO RESPOND

1. Using Handout 16.1: Really Big Questions as a guide, review a few of the questions with the whole class, asking for both answers and brief explanations for the responses given.
2. Read aloud the sample student responses to the questions, "What is the one day of my life I'd relive if I could?" and "What holiday doesn't exist but should?" that are listed on Handout 16.2.
3. Next, ask your students to select one of the questions listed on Handout 16.1 and answer it in large letters on a large sheet of paper. Once completed, you can compile the responses into a classroom book of really big questions.

TIPS TO ENHANCE OR EXTEND THIS LESSON

- If your students enjoyed this lesson, have them compile their own set of big questions and garner responses from both younger and older students at your school. Students could even interview the faculty and staff. If you do video announcements at your school, have one of your students interview a student or adult in response to one of the big questions each day for a week.
- Extend this lesson beyond your classroom and invite the entire school to participate. Start with a question that even young children might be able to answer: *Which fairy tale character would you like to have over for a playdate?* Or, for the children in older grades, tweak this question a bit: *Which historical figure would you most like to interview?* Post selected responses on your class or school website, inviting parents to respond.
- Even though the activities in this book focus on classroom-based interventions, some may work especially well as an introduction to a faculty meeting. Review the big questions on *The Atlantic*'s website and begin a faculty or team meeting by asking teachers and administrators to respond to one of them. This is a fascinating way to learn more about your colleagues, and to listen to the disparate opinions that are likely to emerge.

HANDOUT 16.1

REALLY BIG QUESTIONS

Directions: Just because some questions don't have one correct answer doesn't mean that they are not important questions to ask. Consider how you would respond to the following questions.

1. If you had to put one item into a time capsule that would be opened in 100 years, what object would best represent today's world?

2. What word doesn't exist in our language but should?

3. Which historical figure had the most impact on our world, for good or bad?

4. If you could be a character in a book you've read, who would you be?

5. Which job would you never want to have when you grow up?

6. If you could invent a new color, what would it be?

7. What is the worst prediction ever made that didn't come true?

8. Which child or teenager has made the greatest impact on our world?

9. What is the greatest game ever created?

10. If you could have one superpower, what would it be, and how would you use it?

11. If you were in charge of the world, what is the first thing you would change?

HANDOUT 16.2

SAMPLE RESPONSES

1. What is the one day of my life I'd relive if I could?

   I'd relive the day of my 12th birthday. Instead of the usual cake and ice cream party (although we had those, too) my parents took me to a park near our house. They put a blindfold on me and told me to wait a few minutes. That's when my best friends, my grandparents who live 1,000 miles away, and a kid I grew up with who had moved 2 years ago all came to wish me Happy Birthday. I don't think I've ever been so happy and grateful.

2. What holiday doesn't exist but should?

   I think there should be a holiday to honor relaxation. Everyone seems so busy these days, and even when we have a holiday like the 4th of July or New Year's Eve, people are always planning something to do. My "Relaxation Holiday" would require that people plan absolutely nothing for 24 hours. They just do what they want, even if it's nothing at all.

THE LAST TIME

OBJECTIVE

Students will recall and reflect upon the last time they did something enjoyable or important or felt an emotion strongly.

RESOURCES AND MATERIALS

- Handout 17.1: Interview Questions
- Handout 17.2: Sample Responses
- Faculty colleague to interview

CONTEXT

Before our son took bodily injuries seriously, he was a skateboarder—not a great one but a knock-around, semi-avid one who used his wheeled apparatus at nearby skate parks with similarly inclined friends. He never did airborne tricks and only began wearing knee and elbow pads after an unfortunate event involving concrete. His obsession was short-lived, and that skateboard is now relegated to some obscure basement closet. Once or twice, our son purchased a copy of *Skateboarder Magazine*, trying to perfect a trick or two found within its pages. Not being skateboarding fans ourselves, we had little interest in reading this magazine—except for the last page. On it, there was an interview with a famous skateboarder answering dozens of questions that all began with the same sentence stem, "When was the last time . . . ?" Titled "Last Words," this one-page confessional gave us the idea for this lesson, and it's one that we've been using ever since. After conducting this lesson one time, we think it'll become one of your favorites.

SOCIAL-EMOTIONAL CONNECTIONS

Intimacy and empathy begin with being honest with yourself and being willing to open up emotionally to others. As psychologist Carl Jung stated, "Who looks outside, dreams; who looks inside, awakens." This lesson begins in very safe territory, with students getting to know their classmates' tastes in movies, books and, perhaps, some awards they've won. Pretty quickly, though, the conversations deepen as students discuss their successes, failures, and personal aspirations. The art of listening to one another is a difficult skill to learn, but this activity is one way we've found to help students perfect that most difficult art: seeing the world through someone else's eyes.

THE HOOK

Before class, invite a school colleague (preferably one who knows your students) to visit the classroom. Arrange your students' desks so that they are all facing the middle of your classroom, the place where you and your colleague will sit. Review the questions on Handout 17.1: Interview Questions.

Then, in front of the class, you and your colleague should simply start asking each other whichever questions you'd like. We suggest beginning with some less emotional questions (e.g., "When was the last time you lost something?") and slowly progressing to the more intimate ones (e.g., "When was the last time you felt truly happy?"). As best you can, ignore your students while you simply focus on asking each other these questions. If your students are like ours, they will listen more intently than usual, as they are seeing sides of their teachers they may not have seen before.

After asking 5–7 questions each, turn to your students and say: *Now it's going to be your turn. Find a partner or two and arrange your seats so you can talk to one another and answer some questions like these.*

INVITING STUDENTS TO RESPOND

1. Distribute Handout 17.1: Interview Questions, telling students they will have 10 minutes to ask and answer several of the questions listed. Share several ground rules, including these:
   - ☑ Take turns asking and answering questions.
   - ☑ Be as specific as you can in your responses.
   - ☑ If you wish to *not* answer a question, just say "Pass." A different question will then be asked.
   - ☑ Listen intently and focus your eyes on those of your partner.

2. Once 10 minutes have passed, ask students to give a brief comment to the individual they've just questioned about something new or interesting that they learned from the responses given.

3. Invite students to choose any one of the questions listed and answer it individually in a two- or three-paragraph narrative. If you'd like, you can share with them the responses given by two of our students (see Handout 17.2).

4. Once your students have finished their essays, collect them. For a subsequent class, highlight the questions that were answered most frequently and invite any interested students to share their responses with the class.

TIPS TO ENHANCE OR EXTEND THIS LESSON

- Ask your students to brainstorm additional questions they could ask someone they are trying to get to know better. Compile a master list of these questions and use them in class as journal prompts—*student-initiated* journal prompts.

- If you have student teachers in your school, or your staff contains some new hires, ask them if they are willing to visit your classroom to be interviewed by your students. Have students complete the questions on Handout 17.1: Interview Questions for these individuals. Then, display the responses in a prominent area of your school, complete with a photograph of the individuals who answered these questions.

- Suggest that families do this activity together with your students as an intergenerational "reintroduction" to one another. Including grandparents or college siblings who live away from home in this sharing will encourage emotional connections that are meaningful for everyone involved.

HANDOUT 17.1

INTERVIEW QUESTIONS

1. What was the last book you started but did not finish?

   _____
   _____

2. What was the last award you received?

   _____
   _____

3. When was the last time you lost something?

   _____
   _____

4. What was the last movie you walked out on (or didn't finish)?

   _____
   _____

5. When was the last time you felt out of place?

   _____
   _____

6. When was the last time you felt truly happy?

   _____
   _____

7. When was the last time you were injured?

   _____
   _____

8. When was the last time you felt afraid?

   _____
   _____

NAME: _____ DATE: _____

HANDOUT 17.1, CONTINUED

9. When was the last time you felt respected?

_____

_____

10. When was the last time you failed?

_____

_____

11. When was the last time you felt embarrassed?

_____

_____

12. When was the last time you felt loved?

_____

_____

13. When was the last time you felt totally confused?

_____

_____

14. What was the last good advice you received?

_____

_____

15. What was the last memorable place you visited?

_____

_____

16. When was the last time you wanted to give up?

_____

_____

17. What was the last thing you celebrated?

_____

_____

HANDOUT 17.1, CONTINUED

18. What was your last nightmare?

_____

_____

19. Who was the last person who inspired you?

_____

_____

20. When was the last time you cried?

_____

_____

21. When was the last time you felt envious of someone?

_____

_____

22. When was the last time you laughed?

_____

_____

23. What was the last event that changed your life?

_____

_____

24. When was the last time you made somebody proud?

_____

_____

25. When was the last time you acted silly?

_____

_____

26. Who was the last person who made you feel special?

_____

_____

HANDOUT 17.2

SAMPLE RESPONSES

8. When was the last time you felt afraid?

When I was in third grade, my mom wasn't feeling well and ended up in the hospital for a long time. I didn't know what was happening and when I asked my dad about it, he told me not to worry—that everything would be okay. I know he was trying to make me not worry but his comment only made me feel afraid. I kept thinking he wasn't going to tell me the truth and I also knew he couldn't promise me that my mon would be okay. He wasn't a doctor. I was also afraid because I had said something pretty mean to my mom earlier that day. I was afraid that is the only thing she would remember about me. I felt better when I finally got to see my mom in the hospital and she gave me a big hug. She had a pretty serious issue but eventually she came home and hasn't been sick since. I still get afraid when I think that my mom might not be always around so now I tell her I love her before I go to sleep every night.

23. What was the last event that changed your life?

The last event that changed my life was getting admitted to a school for gifted kids. My attendance here has made me strive to do better and manage my time more. Before I came here, I was very driven, but being a part of a school where almost *everyone* is driven has lit a fire under me. Since the students around me are very intelligent, their successes encourage my own successes. No longer am I the only "smart girl" in class. I'm surrounded by "smart girls" (and boys). I like that. Attending this school has also made me less biased. Since I am exposed to so many different types of people, I have learned to appreciate and not be afraid of people who are different than I am in so many ways.

JUST A LITTLE BIT OF AWESOME

OBJECTIVE

This lesson is designed to help students appreciate the small things in life that make living more fun, more beautiful, or more joyous. Students will compose a short list of small things in life that make each of their days special.

RESOURCES AND MATERIALS

- Handout 18.1: Sample Responses
- (Optional) *The Book of Awesome* by Neil Pasricha (teacher copy)
- (Optional) Video: "The 3 A's of Awesome" by Neil Pasricha (https://www.ted.com/talks/neil_pasricha_the_3_a_s_of_awesome)

CONTEXT

At the end of each school day, when kids run through the door or sit at the dinner table, they are often asked the perennial question, "How was school?" Usually, their responses are quite banal, as spectacular or memorable events seldom happen every day in fifth grade or while rushing from one class to another in an overcrowded middle school hallway. Given that splashy occurrences in school are more rare than common, it's easy for students to fall into the trap of thinking that a particular day was nothing more than ordinary. However, each day *is* pockmarked with tiny incidents that we don't even consider important . . . until we do. In this activity, you will invite your students to consider the smallest things that make life not only more bearable, but also more enjoyable.

SOCIAL-EMOTIONAL CONNECTIONS

Too often, kids and adults alike don't take the time to consider the smallest things that bring a smile to their faces or give them hope. However, if we take just a few moments to focus on those often-ignored moments of fun, joy, and revelation, the world can seem less scary and, perhaps, just a little more beautiful. For people who often see their emotional glass as half empty instead of half full, this lesson can have a positive effect on well-being and social relationships. It will help your kids realize that they choose their responses to situations, even when bad things happen. They get to choose to be optimistic or pessimistic.

THE HOOK

Share a true story that ties directly into this lesson. You may use or adapt the following story or share another related to an athlete, artist, soldier, etc. (*Note.* This example is better for older students; you will need to adapt it for younger students.)

> In 2006, life was great for Canadian Neil Pasricha (2010). A recent college graduate now gainfully employed, Neil had also just gotten married and was enjoying the happy and fulfilling life he was leading. When he was a child, Neil's parents emigrated from Kenya and India to give him a comfortable life that they themselves never expected to experience in their newly adopted country. All was right with the world—until it wasn't.
>
> A couple of years after they were married, Neil's wife came home from work one day to tell him she didn't love him anymore. Divorce followed. Added to that, Neil's best friend, who had been suffering from depression, chose to end his life. Neil was at an emotional crossroad: He had to decide if he was going to wallow in his grief and pain, or if he could move forward and try to establish a new life filled with more joy than sadness. His answer was the latter: He moved ahead.

Neil began writing a blog, "1000 Awesome Things" (http://1000awesomethings.com), where he related simple, everyday happenings that brought a smile to his face, like smelling bakery air, finding money in the pocket of an old jacket, getting a smile from a stranger as you approach one another on a hiking path, watching grandparents dance with their grandchildren, or going to a grocery store and having a new cashier line open up just as you're about to check out. His blog started small but has now been viewed more than 10 million times. Neil's simple idea of finding the small things that make life more enjoyable became a best-selling book, *The Book of Awesome*, followed by additional volumes of awesome things. Neil even shared a TED Talk that has been viewed by millions of people. Making lemonade out of lemons paid off mightily, in many ways, for Neil Pasricha.

After you have shared this story, your student will probably know the focus of this writing lesson: to write about some of the small things that are easy to ignore but, if they *aren't* ignored, can make for a happier, more fulfilling life.

INVITING STUDENTS TO RESPOND

1. If you have access to Neil Pasricha's book or wish to show his TED Talk, either would be a great way to introduce your students to their writing assignment. However, neither is necessary if you have introduced this activity using the suggestions in The Hook section.
2. Instruct students to come up with 3–5 awesome things that are everyday occurrences, followed by a brief description of what makes each of these small things awesome.
3. Distribute Handout 18.1: Sample Responses to help students generate ideas.

TIPS TO ENHANCE OR EXTEND THIS LESSON

- If you teach this lesson early in the school year, you can follow it up at the end of the school year by focusing on "Five Awesome Things About School This Year." For older students, ask them to consider "Five Awesome Things That Happened in Our World This Year," which, given all of the hardships that individuals and nations endure in any given year, might put a positive spin on the world's future prospects.

- Instead of focusing on life in general, ask your students to select an important individual in their lives and write "Five Awesome Things About _____." This person could be a parent, a friend, a teacher, a grandparent, etc. Encourage students to share their list of awesome attributes with that person.

- Ask your students to imagine their futures and write "Five Awesome Things About My Life at Age 40." What will they have done? Who will they have met? What goals will they still hope to accomplish? Once completed, return the "wish lists" to your students and tell them to keep them in a place that they will remember decades from now.

- Have students self-address envelopes and seal their awesome lists within. Then, tell them you will mail them in a certain number of years. (*Note.* It might take a little bit of tenacity on your part to remember to mail the letters. One idea: Have students jot down a date on the envelopes so you can keep track of when to mail them.)

HANDOUT 18.1

SAMPLE RESPONSES

Student 1

1. **When you go on a website to watch a show, and no popups open.** There are days when you just *have* to use a website to watch that latest movie or TV show. If you find a website with no popups, you've hit a goldmine.

2. **When it starts raining right after you get into your car.** I love wearing my rain jacket, but, if you're dressed nicely, it can mess up your look. So, it's awesome when the rain starts only after you've gotten into a car, so you didn't have to put on the rain jacket at all.

3. **When your phone is about to fall, and you catch it at the last second.** Every time my phone falls, I have a heart thump. So, when I'm as fast as light speed and I catch my phone before it hits the ground, I'm like "ooooh . . . I can't believe I just did that!"

Student 2

1. **That whisper you get when you open your bottle of soda.** Everyone knows that sound—the little "pssst" when you first open your cola bottle. It's magnificent. It is saying, "Hello, I am your drink. Enjoy me." It is one of the most refreshing sounds *ever*.

2. **When two book characters finally confess their feelings for each other.** We all know that annoying, long build-up of characters who were meant to be with one another. We all wait and wait for one of them to just come out and say how they feel. Every good love story has these moments—and they are truly magnificent when they happen!

3. **A comfortable silence.** With the right people, silence is comfortable, not awkward. This silence means that you know each other so well that you don't need to talk. You can just sit there and feel immersed in comfort.

Student 3

1. **When you tell a joke that's not funny, but people laugh anyway.** So . . . you tell a joke that's not really funny and you expect no one to laugh . . . but they do anyway. That shows that they are good friends.

HANDOUT 18.1, CONTINUED

2. **When you see a dog and get to pet it.** You're at a beach or walking down a street and you see this *amazingly* cute dog walking toward you. Your heart immediately jumps, and, as you get closer, you ask the owner if you can pet the dog. That becomes 20 seconds of pure happiness.

3. **When you do well on a test you didn't study for.** I'm sure everyone has had a test that they totally forgot about having to take. You enter class feeling that inevitable failure awaits you. When you return to class the next day and find that you didn't bomb the test, you feel both relieved and *awesome.*

4. **When you finally become a friend.** Although you may talk to a person a lot, they might not trust you at first. It takes a while to build up that trust. When I manage to finally build up enough trust with this person and I can finally call them a friend, I realize that I now have someone I can depend on. That's *awesome!*

IF WE WERE IN CHARGE OF THE WORLD

OBJECTIVE

In this lesson, students identify specific world concerns and solutions to these concerns, and then present their ideas in group-generated poems.

RESOURCES AND MATERIALS

- Handout 19.1: Sample Response
- Poem: "If I Were in Charge of the World" by Judith Viorst (https://www.poemhunter.com/poem/if-i-were-in-charge-of-the-world)

CONTEXT

Begin this lesson with a premise: Many kids believe they could do a better job at running our world than the adults who are now in charge. This lesson gives students the chance to make their ideas known. Using Judith Viorst's poem "If I Were in Charge of the World" as their model, students will combine their creativity and talents to create their own poetic version of how different the world might be if kids were in charge. Because the poem is generated from the combined efforts and voices of multiple students, the final product reflects at least a little bit of each student's contribution.

SOCIAL-EMOTIONAL CONNECTIONS

In today's world of instant communication, whatever happens in our world, for better or worse, is broadcast to everyone at the same time. In previous generations, adults learned about tragedies before they shared the news with children, if, indeed, they shared it at all. Now, thanks to the Internet and smartphones that give instant access to news, the greatest triumphs and the saddest occurrences hit both children and adults simultaneously. For many sensitive kids, this can be a scary situation, as they may not be equipped emotionally to handle the barrage of incidents that seem to hit our smartphone screens nonstop. By giving kids the chance to express their own hopes for the world, we allow them to articulate some messages that they might otherwise keep to themselves. Additionally, students come to see themselves as problem solvers, and they can build on the critical attribute of being a caring and productive citizen of the world in later activities.

THE HOOK

As your students gather for the day, ask if any of them have ever been "the boss"—the person in charge of something. Elicit some specific examples of situations in which students have been in charge (e.g., the captain of a sports team, the section leader in choir or band, or a babysitter). Ask what some of the benefits are of being in charge (e.g., "People have to do what I tell them to do"), followed by some of the responsibilities of being in charge (e.g., "If things don't turn out right, I'll be the one to get blamed"), as well as some of the drawbacks (e.g., "You probably have less time for yourself, because you're trying to help other people succeed"). At this point, extend the questioning to ask how the world would be different if the students were in charge. What would they change? What would they keep the same? What would they like to see improved?

After you've gathered a few responses, read Judith Viorst's poem aloud, eliciting comments about specific lines in the poem that students like or dislike.

INVITING STUDENTS TO RESPOND

1. Tell students that it is now their turn to improve the world by composing some ideas on how to make it a better place.

129

2. Divide your students into groups of 4–6. Explain that each group will generate ideas about how students would change the world to improve it. To encourage thoughtful brainstorming, suggest to students that they think of both humorous and serious ideas for improving the world.

3. Ask one student in each group to serve as a recorder of the ideas given. Allow about 10–15 minutes for this brainstorming.

4. Before asking students to share some of their ideas based on Viorst's poem, show them the poem created by sixth graders on Handout 19.1: Sample Response. Mention again the mixture of serious and humorous thoughts and encourage your students to include both as they prepare to compose their own poems. Mention, too, that not *every* idea should be included in the group poem, but that input should be sought from every student.

5. When all groups have completed their poems, have them share with the rest of the class.

TIPS TO ENHANCE OR EXTEND THE LESSON

- Once your small groups of students have created and shared their poems, take the poems home and compile a class poem that includes several ideas from each of the small groups. Leave space at the bottom of the page, where students can sign their names as a class commitment to make the world a better place.

- This activity works really well if done with an entire team or grade level, not just one classroom. Not only do you receive a greater variety of responses, but by combining voices from dozens and dozens of children, you provide an even greater sense of togetherness and camaraderie.

- Share the compositions with the art teacher in your school and ask if the students can illustrate their poems as a poster project activity. The resulting posters can be displayed throughout the school, adding fun, energy, and thoughtfulness to any hallway or doorway they adorn.

HANDOUT 19.1

SAMPLE RESPONSE

Class Poem, Grade 6

If We Were in Charge of the World

If we were in charge of the world,
all drinking fountains would be filled with Dr. Pepper,
candy would clean your teeth like toothpaste,
and McDonald's food would have no calories.

If we were in charge of the world,
homework would be outlawed,
we'd study from comic books,
and teachers who gave too many tests would get suspended from school.

If we were in charge of the world,
kids couldn't call you names you didn't like,
but if they did, they'd have to apologize and make up with you.
Parents would have to eat Brussels sprouts twice each week,
and they'd have to go to bed when their kids told them to.

If we were in charge of the world,
people who polluted a beautiful place would have to pay to clean it up,
garbage dumps would be replaced with trash-eating plants,
and all the bamboo forests in China would be restored.

If we were in charge of the world,
no hungry or needy people would exist,
every nation would be at peace,
and people everywhere would always understand what you are trying to say emotionally.
If we were in charge of the world.

IT GIVES ME . . .

OBJECTIVE

This lesson allows students to capture impressions of their lives in short, meaningful phrases or sentences.

RESOURCES AND MATERIALS

* Handout 20.1: It Gives Me . . .
* Handout 20.2: Sample Responses

CONTEXT

It was the last day of the school year in Jim Delisle's classroom. Field Day had just ended, and a bunch of now-sweaty eighth graders anticipated coming back to the classroom to do little more than sign yearbooks and count down the clock until summer vacation began. But first, Jim had one final writing exercise to complete.

"Huh?" sighed this collective group of students. "*Another* writing activity?"

The answer was "yes," and if there is a better way to end a school year than by completing this lesson, we haven't yet found it.

SOCIAL-EMOTIONAL CONNECTIONS

The end of a school year is generally filled with a range of emotions for everyone involved. Whether the year was an exciting one filled with new learning adventures, or a "let me count down the days until it's over" year because of multiple challenges, the approximately 180-day bond between teachers and their students is one that few other professions share. So, as the year's end approaches, it is good to reflect on those moments of hope, joy, and pride, and to pause for a few moments of quiet thought as well. This lesson allows teachers and their students to end even the most difficult year on a positive and forward-looking note. Encouraging students to self-reflect allows them to gain an appreciation for their personal growth as well as to understand how their responses impact their lives and the lives of others. Additionally, reflection allows students to dream—and what better lesson in life is there?

THE HOOK

OK, we admit it: Getting kids hooked on a writing project as the school year is nanoseconds away from ending can be challenging. Therefore, your approach to presenting this lesson is going to make or break your students' reactions to it. So, proceed cautiously!

Here's what we do: First of all, we hold a brief class discussion on how students' day has gone, asking them to highlight just one brief example of something funny or touching that happened during Field Day (or however you spend your last day together in school). It could be one of the more athletic kids falling in the mud during the tug-of-war, or another student who helped a child with special needs race across the finish line during the relay race. The content of their memories isn't as important as the tone this sharing helps to set: *We've been in this class together all year—laughing, crying, striving.*

Banking on the range of emotions that usually accompanies emerging adolescence, tell students that you are asking them to do some personal reflecting on their lives at this point in time. They may appreciate engaging in an activity that doesn't have right or wrong answers! These short statements will include personal anecdotes that speak to their hopes, joys, aspirations, or continuing questions about life in general. If they are still unconvinced that a writing activity on the last day of school can be meaningful, and they send you those leery looks that young adolescents have perfected, then turn on the guilt: *Come on . . . one last writing activity. I promise never to do this to you again.* Your humor and honesty will help generate their own.

INVITING STUDENTS TO RESPOND

1. Distribute Handout 20.1: It Gives Me . . . and ask your students to write four items for each of the categories listed: joy, hope, pride, and pause.

2. If you need to prime their mental pumps with a few examples, you can share several of the examples provided by our students (see Handout 20.2). Don't provide too many examples, but just enough to get your students' thoughts going.

3. After 10–15 minutes (at most), roam around the room, stopping at individuals' desks and stating one of the prompts. For example, when you approach Laquisha's desk, simply look at her and say, "It gives me joy . . ." to which she will read out loud something she wrote to complete this statement.

4. Do this with several more students, before inviting anyone else to complete the statements as you read the four stems—joy, hope, pride, pause. Continue doing so until student responses ebb.

5. Once students have completed their responses, ask them one final question: *Why do you think I had you complete this assignment?* You'll likely hear a couple of "I was wondering the same thing" comments, but those will be followed with some more sincere, thoughtful observations: "To think about our lives and what's important to us" or "To let you know what's going on in our minds."

6. End this lesson with nothing more than a sincere "thank you" and best wishes for continued fun and learning in the years ahead.

TIPS TO ENHANCE OR EXTEND THIS LESSON

- If you wish to extend this lesson beyond the last-day suggestion provided, have students complete the same four prompts—joy, hope, pride, pause—from the point of view of a historical or scientific figure they've studied or a fictional character from one of their favorite books. It might just add a new layer of complexity to the standard book report.

- You can make this an intergenerational lesson by asking your students to ask important people in their lives—parents, siblings, friends, grandparents, other family members—to complete the four prompts. Then, students can compare each of these four prompts, considering the age ranges of the people who gave them.

By comparing a 10-year-old sister's responses with those of a 70-year-old grandmother, students can find both commonalities and distinctions among the most influential people in their lives.

- Introduce the artwork and ideas of author Candy Chang (2013) to your students. (*Note.* This activity might not be appropriate for younger students, so know your audience.) Author Candy Chang, whose mother died when Candy was 15 years old, was grief-stricken for all of the expected reasons. She felt sad that her mother never experienced many of the things she had hoped to do in life: live in Paris, see the Pacific Ocean, dance with her grandchildren. Candy's solution was to create artwork in which the canvas was chalkboard paint, allowing people to write directly on it. She took this idea worldwide, painting buildings with chalkboard paint in Thailand, America, Costa Rica and elsewhere, inviting strangers to complete the phrase "Before I die, I want to . . ." Each night, the "canvases" were erased, and each new morning, people came back and finished this phrase. Chang's internationally recognized work is documented in her book *Before I Die*, which features hundreds of hopes, dreams, and aspirations from people young and old alike. Although the thought of death is not one that you want to raise with young children, introducing Candy Chang's artwork and ideas to adolescents is something we have done successfully and thoughtfully. One alternate extension can be: *Things to do before I am fifty*. As a tie-in to this activity, Chang's book takes this idea to a deeper, more introspective level.

HANDOUT 20.1

IT GIVES ME . . .

Directions: Reflect on the times when you felt joy, hope, pride, and pause. List four items for each category.

It Gives Me Joy . . .

_____

_____

_____

_____

It Gives Me Hope . . .

_____

_____

_____

_____

It Gives Me Pride . . .

_____

_____

_____

_____

It Gives Me Pause . . .

_____

_____

_____

_____

SAMPLE RESPONSES

It Gives Me Joy . . .

- when I make babies laugh.
- when friends come up behind me and put their hands over my eyes and make me guess who it is.
- when I finish a good book and see the world from the eyes of a character in it.
- when people give me the kindness I deserve rather than treating me as if I am not popular.
- when I read Maya Angelou's poem "Phenomenal Woman."
- when I hear preschoolers singing their ABC's.
- when my brother gives me a ride to school happily, with no complaints.
- when I wake up on a summer morning, greeted by the sun, and realize that this day has the potential to be the best one of my life.

It Gives Me Hope . . .

- when I see a friend succeed in something I helped her learn.
- when I think of my parents still being alive when I am an adult.
- when I see a very biased person change his mind.
- when I see my mother going through so much and still being strong and never hanging her head in shame.
- when I see my grandmother and she still remembers who I am.
- when I know I can talk to my sister about anything.
- when my mom says "see you later" instead of "goodbye."

It Gives Me Pride . . .

- when I understand something I have been struggling with.
- when my sister dances.
- when my favorite team, the Chicago White Sox, wins a game.
- when I finally learn to do a trick on my skateboard that I've been practicing for weeks.
- when I act like the good person that I am.
- when I represent well my family, school, or town.
- when I get treated like the young adult I will soon become.

HANDOUT 20.2, CONTINUED

It Gives Me Pause . . .

- when I think about the universe and my place in it.
- when I lose my homework.
- when I look at the world's problems and wonder how I can change them.
- when I think about how fast my life is flying by—I'm 13 already!
- when I think that one day the world will be in my generation's hands.
- when I think of a million questions that have no answers.
- when I consider how many people struggle with something that is easy for me.
- when I think about how happy I am with myself; it's actually quite remarkable!

REFERENCES

Barkley, K. M. (2016). *8 reasons why poetry is good for the soul*. Retrieved from https://www.writersdigest.com/whats-new/8-reasons-why-poetry-is-good-for-the-soul

Belfield, C., Bowden, B., Klapp, A., Levin, H., Shand, R., & Zander. S. (2015). *The economic value of social and emotional learning*. New York, NY: Teachers College Press.

Chang, C. (2013). *Before I die*. New York, NY: St. Martin's Griffin.

Collaborative for Academic, Social, and Emotional Learning. (2018). *What is SEL?* Retrieved from https://casel.org/what-is-sel

Elias, M. J., Ferrito, J. J., & Moceri, D. C. (2016). *The other side of the report card: Assessing students social, emotional, and character development*. Thousand Oaks, CA: Corwin.

Long, D. (2012). *The fool who invented kissing* [E-reader version]. Retrieved from http://fictivepress.com/the-fool-who-invented-kissing.htm

Looney, A. (1999–2000). *Nanofiction*. Retrieved from http://www.wunder land.com/WTS/Andy/Nanofiction.html

Pasricha, N. (2010). The 3 A's of awesome [Video file]. *TED*. Retrieved from https://www.ted.com/talks/neil_pasricha_the_3_a_s_of_awesome

Ramsey, A. (2018). *Profundity in Portland* [Web log post]. Retrieved from https://www.andrearamsey.com/profundity-in-portland

Zins, J. E, Bloodworth, M. R., Weissberg, R. P., & Walberg, H. J. (2004). "The scientific base linking social and emotional learning to school success." In J. Zins, R. P. Weissberg, M. C. Wang, & A. J. Walberg (Eds.), *Building academic success on social and emotional learning: What does the research say?* (pp. 3–22). New York, NY: Teachers College Press.

ABOUT THE AUTHORS

Deborah S. Delisle is the president and CEO of the Alliance for Excellent Education (All4Ed), a national nonprofit committed to improving the educational outcomes—and lives—of high school students, especially those who are underperforming and historically underserved. She previously served as the executive director and CEO of ASCD, an international nonprofit organization with 120,000 members across 128 countries whose primary mission is to provide high-quality products, services, and professional development to educators at all levels.

James R. Delisle, Ph.D., has been an educator of children with disabilities and those who are gifted for more than 40 years. As a teacher, professor, author, and dad, Jim has focused his work on the social and emotional development of children. Jim has written 23 books and has been a consultant for schools throughout the world, including such diverse nations as Thailand, New Zealand, Oman, Germany, China, and others.